7 Types of Queens,
Kings Desire

To Queen Avah Allen,

Many Blessings to

you & your family!
Inspiration!

12/1/2014

King Kevin Dorival

Published by Sky View Creative Circle, LLC.

Editor: Kendra Applewhite of Kym Writes
Book Cover Design: Raphael "Cano" Colon
Interior Book Design: Jose Pepito Jr.

ISBN: 978-0-9855648-3-4

First Printing July 2017

For information on special discounts for bulk purchases, please contact:
King Kevin Dorival at 7queens7kings@gmail.com
Or visit his website at www.7queens7kings.com
Mailing Address: P.O. Box 667136, Pompano Beach, FL 33066

1. Self-Help & Relationships > Love & Romance >
History > Ethnic Cultures > Nonfiction.

CONTENTS

ABOUT THE COVER

*E*ven though there are only seven women on the book cover, it was meant to represent all cultures. I had to think long and hard to handpick the queens I felt were most important to society. Some of these women stuck out to me, such as the First Lady Michelle Obama, Florence Delorez Griffith Joyner, and Princess Diana. I wanted young girls to pick up the book and to think very highly of themselves and of their capabilities to improve the world. I wanted grown women to pick up the book and to be elated. When these ladies pick up the book, it is my desire that the appeal of the book will make them smile and that they will inevitably want to read a page or two.

The history within the book had to be portrayed on the cover. This is why Queen Auset was placed on the cover with the Northern Crown of Kemet (today's Egypt), represented by the cobra on the front of the crown. Queen Hatshepsut was one of the most powerful women in the ancient world. She was one of the rare women (possibly one of four female rulers) who ruled as a pharaoh during the eighteenth dynasty of Kemet, the most powerful civilization in the world during that time in Africa. Queen Hatshepsut was the longest-serving indigenous female pharaoh in Egypt.

The traditions of the Geisha had to be included in my book, as well. I have too much respect for the Asian dynasties and style of their traditions. The heart shape of all the women epitomizes that the true crown of a woman is her heart. It's not a crown, a scepter, or fancy robe – it's the love energy that is projected into the universe.

DEDICATION

*T*his book is dedicated to my mother, Queen Rosette Pierre. She is the queen of all queens in my life. I wish you were here to witness your son release his second book. It wouldn't have been possible without your grace and love all over me. I would like to dedicate the motivation for writing this book to my forthcoming wife, the mother of my future children.

In honor of our mother, my family is hopeful that the Queen Rosette Pierre Scholarship will be available for single mothers and fathers from the Caribbean who desire to attend school. The funds will pay for childcare and/or books to help ease the financial burden that comes with seeking a higher education ($1,000 or more, per student). Growing up, my mother couldn't find anyone in our family to babysit us, so she had to quit cosmetology school. For every purchase of this book, two dollars will go toward The Queen Rosette Pierre Scholarship (under the 501(c) 3, non-fiction organization Courage To Believe International).

I would also like to give honor and recognition to all the women of the past and present who have tapped into their divine feminine powers.

FOREWORD

"What type of Queen are you?"

The King/Queen theme is dear to my heart, as I believe we all can become one. We are all gods and goddesses, but to become a King or a Queen, we must reach our highest level of consciousness (located at the *crown* Chakra). At this point, there's nothing we cannot achieve together!

7 Types of Queens, Kings Desire will help you identify your Queen type, in order to help you attract your ideal King. Knowing how to identify a King from a frog will save you tons of wasted time and energy, while preventing repeated heartache.

"King" Kevin Dorival takes you on a journey of self-discovery to identify your Queen-type. Prepare to take on the spiritual role you should play in the lives of those around you – especially your King!

Throughout this book you will study great Queens from the past, such as:

- Queen Nzinga

- Harriet Tubman

- Queen Candace

- Winnie Mandela

- Queen Auset

- First Lady Michelle Obama

By studying the lives of great Queens from the past such as Queen Nzinga, Harriet Tubman, Queen Candace, Afeni Shakur, Mother Teresa, Winnie Mandela, Queen Auset, and the First Lady Michelle Obama, you will learn how to assist the King in your life to MANifest his desires. Yet, this is not all one-sided. Kings and Queens must serve each other! If you seek to cultivate a relationship that is healthy, long-term, fulfilling, and loving — a healthy, fulfilling, loving, long-term relationship, there are certain qualities you must possess or obtain. King Kevin Dorival will show you how powHERful your words are, which can build your man up. Your words can help resurrect him to Kingly status (or break him down). Making your home a throne for your King is also a part of a woman's Queenly duties. Including spiritual practices, such as praying for (and with) him, will assist in cultivating a bond between both of you. Furthermore, knowing how to keep his eyes from straying (as men are visual creatures) is also part of your Queenly charms.

Once you identify what type of Queen you are, you can best know what type of King you wish to attract! Allow me to help you build a solid foundation to your lasting empire and your relationship!

Queen Cezanne Taharqa

INTRODUCTION

"Mothers are the bread of life, the milk of renewed
strength, the one that not only fed you but clothes
you as well." – Dr. Ishakamusa Barashango

It's been asked: *What made you write a book about women?* To be honest, I wrote this book after my heart was broken and shattered by a young lady. I thought I was in love with this Queen for the long ride, but as time revealed, this relationship was not the right fit for me. I couldn't believe she wanted to remove herself from our picture-perfect world. As a man of valor, I was ready to give her half of my kingdom while showing her off to the world. On the outside, she looked fit for a king. Internally, however, her world was a dungeon begging to be cleansed of the foul spirits from past relationship pains that quietly tormented her. Unbeknownst to me, she was silently screaming that she was not ready to jump the broom. I fell from our "Love Plane" after this realization. Love gave me a natural high I'd never experienced prior to this relationship.

Before my broken heart healed, I began to write about my pain, my frustration, and my world without her sunshine. I eventually snapped out of it, but it gave me valuable energy and content for the book you are about to read.

This book was originally a dating manual for spiritually strong people trying to keep it holy through celibacy before marriage; this, however, is very difficult for many. After the breakup, I redirected my energy toward finding the perfect woman for me. As you open this treasure chest of knowledge, be prepared to unlock the answer to the question:

What type of Queen am I?

As *7 Types of Queens, Kings Desire* began to take flight, I realized I had something special on my hands. I became conscious that this was going to be an extraordinary book on the horizon. This book will foster solid relationships, communities, and rock-solid parenting skills. It will create more fulfilling marriages by empowering both women and men. I've come to understand that we can't just tell people something is important; rather, we need to show them. It helps to bring the message home. Comprehension is a beautiful thing. It is needed for the future of our children. Without it, we could face a tomorrow where everyone is detached from the real world — a society dependent upon text messages, emails, and social media as the only means of building and sustaining relationships. This book aims to fight for our daughters' consciousness, dignity, and self-respect.

Additionally, there are many aspects that a great woman brings into a relationship: wisdom, grace, love, home-cooked meals for the soul, and so forth. The feminine energy has the power to manifest everything that it places within its heart. Most men must try extra hard to internalize things, unless it becomes an enemy and a threat to what they care about. As you read these pages, you will learn about some of the greatest women who have walked on this planet. Some of them found their greatest strengths leading wars against invading nations, while others are powerful game changers in the corporate world. All of them have one thing in common: they found their awesomeness in their divine feminine energy and innate powers as a woman!

In truth, having sex, sensual dancing, and home-cooked meals at the dinner table are sacred ceremonial traditions that have lasted thousands of years, but society has transformed them into hobbies or pastimes. Nowadays, people are just satisfied with eating fast food, juicy text messages, and quickies. An African proverb states: "We must go back and reclaim our past so we can move forward; so that we understand why and how we came to be who we are today."

Today, our world needs more successful, loving marriages. This, in turn, will supply our youth with great examples of what defines a good marriage and a happy home. Why focus on marriages and not just great relationships? Marriage requires commitment. It takes time to cultivate a marriage and it brings families together. Most importantly, a great marriage adds light to the community. This is composed of good communication, teamwork, sacrifices, compromises, morals, and loyalty.

Having a lasting marriage isn't the answer to all our societal problems, but I firmly believe it will alleviate many difficulties we face today. Everyone under this union will be groomed for excellence. Goddesses, gods, queens, mothers, fathers, kings, daughters, and sons will have a better chance to be the best version of themselves. When a union takes place between two gods representing the feminine and masculine principles, they'll be able to create anything the two of them place their minds and energies toward.

During my studies, I researched several types of queens that powerful kings desired, specifically African kings like pharaoh Akhenaten of ancient Egypt (1353 B.C.-1362 B.C.), and the husband of Queen Nefertiti. Furthermore, I studied queens and kings all the way up to the 44th President of the United States: Barack Obama and First Lady Michelle Obama. Based on the questions and discussions that I've had over multiple years with happily married men and proud bachelors, I've produced some very interesting perspectives.

Throughout history, many of the greatest ideas of the world manifested from the inspiration of women behind the scenes. Coretta Scott King pushed Dr. Martin Luther King, Jr. to march from Selma to Montgomery, Alabama. King Xerxes built one of the seven wonders of the ancient world, The Hanging Gardens, for his Queen Amyitis. These are just two examples out of many great accomplishments motivated by the feminine energy. A third example came from a series on the *King Kevin Show* episode about what men desire in a relationship and what they look for in a wife with the Queen Code™. When part three of the show came around, titled *7 Types of Queens, Kings Desire*, the idea to write a book on the subject hit me like a treasure chest of blessings. Mrs. Crawford of the Queen Code played a significant role in pushing me in this direction. She wouldn't allow me to be quiescent with an idea as hot as this one.

I thank God for women like her who see the hidden greatness in most men, pull it out of them, and bring it into existence. This is the quintessence of a woman's role to her man and to her community. The same goes for a man's role toward his queen.

Single, good women yearn to know the answers to the following questions: *What do good men desire from women? How can I become the queen of my king's dreams without sacrificing my uniqueness as a woman?* And, most interestingly, how can I get a king to court me without telling him directly? These are valid questions and, to be honest, Google, Facebook, nor the internet can answer them. Only your spirit can reveal the answers. If you're wondering: How can my spirit lead me to my soul mate, my king, or my destiny? It's going to require some deep down, real-life soul searching to find your soul mate and king or to allow your soul mate to find you. You may have to reduce the amount of clutter, cosmetics, and distractions surrounding you. Your spirit will need a chance to breathe in and breathe out.

SPIRIT AND ENERGIES

Because I'm going to use the terms spirit and energy frequently throughout this book, I will explain what they mean to me. Allow me to give you this caveat first. I'm not promoting any religions or denouncing them. I'm going to simply state historically proven information. However, I will explain my belief system.

The spirit consists of unified energy forces that transport intelligence. Society should not confuse it with magic or ghosts. Some people have a foul spirit, while others have a righteous one. This is also true of one's energy. There are too many spirits to name, and I will explain several types of spirits women once possessed in abundance during times of antiquity. After all, my focus will remain on the positive and beauteous types of spirits. This book was designed to be a blessing for your spirit and mind. My intention is to bring you to a higher level of consciousness, while teaching you solutions to issues single women encounter today. Additionally, I will provide solid solutions in order to adopt higher standards for your relationship goals.

There are men roaming the earth who are sent by the enemy. They try and break you down which, in turn, pulls you from the seat of your throne. These males eagerly try to diminish your light. This book will guide you through history and teach you how to deflect males that carry this type of negative spirit and energy. Some of you have been trying to figure out how to understand the aforementioned. Contrary to popular belief, the roles many women have been taught, your role in life, and your power aren't limited to the kitchen or the bedroom. It is channeling the energy God blessed each and every one of you with to give birth to ideas and new life. As a woman, you have the life-giving power—naturally. This should not be taken for granted.

Ladies, queens, and mademoiselles — at some point in your life you will have to determine what type of woman you are. Then, figure out what type of queen you want to become before you settle down. A man won't appreciate you if you don't embrace your qualities first. You're going to have to conduct some serious soul searching. Take the time to analyze your strengths, and acknowledge your weaknesses so that you can work to improve them. By recognizing your power, you've already won half the battle.

Queen Auset and First Lady Michelle Obama carry the same sovereign love energy that every man of vision seeks. I want you to find the level of your love energy, and then increase it until you reach full capacity. This will enable you to catch your *love plane* in stride with the man that you're destined to be with, rather than whom you choose to be with due to desperation. A *love plane* is created by the synchrony and harmony of two people involved with each other. You can evaluate and uplift your relationship to higher heights. The sky is the limit.

The frequencies and vibrations of people are like radio station airwaves. Some airwaves are clean, clear, and a pleasure to tune into, while others are fuzzy and require a lot of work to understand. This, in turn, makes communication difficult. It drains you of energy. On the other hand, there are stations which you should simply give up on. You will never be able to understand their frequency to comprehend what is being communicated to you. The latter will cause you to constantly lower your frequency level (your energy) to communicate with a particular person. The next thing you know, the people in your circle won't be able to understand why your light has dimmed or they'll wonder what happened to the aura they once admired. Usually, the only people who can get close enough to dim our light are those we have a relationship with: family members, boyfriends, husbands, coworkers, and/or neighbors.

Check for vibrations (vibes) of those around you on a regular basis, as if you are a walking thermometer reading the temperament of everyone around you. Vibrations are the auras of an individual. The infectious smile of a person projects a positive vibration, while a frown gives a depressed or negative vibration. Surround yourself with those who keep your vibrations high. Discard those who diminish your vibe; they serve no purpose in your life. If you never saw or spoke to them again, would it impact your life?

You will learn how to focus your invisible energy to wake up the righteous queen in you.

What's more, there is a divine alignment between the feminine and masculine energies. These are known as our spirits. It's like a car having two flats on the same side, and then finally pumping air into both tires to fix the flat. Do you think the car began to drive just a little or a lot faster to its destination? The air in your tires represents your energy. There are people sent to deflate your energy. Notice how some people take a lot more effort to deal with than others; you have to prepare yourself to interact with them. Otherwise, it's better to avoid them by any means necessary. Many women are in relationships with men who are the antithesis of love and positive energy. You could end up in a dispirited union for the rest of your life. I'm here to encourage you so that the chances are slim that this will happen.

I wrote this book for women, young and old, all over the world. My hope is that it empowers these women with wisdom, power, and knowledge. As a result, they will apply this information into their lives. What will follow is that your husband, or soon-to-be-king, will tremendously benefit from it. Knowledge is food to the brain, just as water contains vital nutrients for flowers and plants: the more you know, the more you grow and blossom.

A woman who can stimulate her mind will stimulate her man as well. This stimulation will last longer than any bedroom episode. Cavemen will hate this book due to their male chauvinistic dogma. On the other hand, a modern man would appreciate the knowledge and research placed into this book. In fact, he will appreciate having a woman who aligns with what most great men desire in a queen.

We all can rule and reign with the life we've been given on earth. There is no reason we should struggle to have faith in the Creator and what has been promised to us, including:

- God's promise to bring you a king worthy of your presence

- power

- grace

- energy

This king will fight for your honor, contend for the future family you two will create, and protect your new world of blessings.

WHY THE NUMBER SEVEN

The number seven represents divine connection. It's the number of perfection and divine completion. According to the Bible, God rested on the seventh day. There are seven seas, seven continents, and seven Chakras. In Japan, there are Seven Lucky Gods. The spectrum is divided into seven colors, and seven colors make up a rainbow. There are seven major parts of the heart and brain and seven layers to our skin. Our body replaces all cells every seven years. The Seventh Heaven comes from a divine completion. Jesus was said to have made seven statements before he died on the cross. If the number seven was important to The Creator, then it should be important to you and I. The 7-Eleven convenience store was founded in 1927. I was born on the 7th of February.

Ladies, you will either establish or increase your king-building capabilities. Most men must build something in their lives to feel adequate; without you, it will be impossible. This book will infuse you with knowledge of handpicked queens who paved the way from the ancient world to modern times. Increasing your consciousness will be your responsibility. I am just a humble messenger guiding you in the right direction.

Thanks for supporting me, and I hope you enjoy the *7 Types of Queens, Kings Desire*.

CHAPTER 1

MOTHER GOD

The thought of the Creator being addressed
as Mother God may be shocking to many,
but this is how "God" the Creator was
originally worshipped in ancient times.

The Mother God was venerated because the main source of trade and stability was agriculture related to fertility. The role of the woman changed along with society. As wars became more frequent, the world became a male-dominated society. This was also factual for the deities. Our true powers are in the unseen world, which is where our spirits are fighting or giving up on battles that we cannot see with our physical eyes. Our intuition can sense when something good or bad is happening. The trick is to be in tune with your spirit. This is the god within you. Don't be afraid. Believe in the Creator and the Creator's power inside of you. To be truly robust and reclaim your divine power as Mother Goddess, you must follow the laws of nature to assist you in purification, thereby becoming one with the Most High's almighty power.

With a balanced life, diet, personal and impersonal skills, temperance, prudence, purity, and self-control — you'll be on your way to reach sophrosyne. This is an ancient Greek concept representing an ideal of excellence within soundness and character of mind. Our society today needs our queens back on their throne now more than ever. Homes are in disarray; the men are running aimlessly everywhere except to their families.

Many ancient traditions, such as in Alkebulan (known as Africa today), believed all answers to our problems could be found from within. Many of our women today are operating in a spirit of fear. The most dangerous type of person to encounter is one consumed with fear. Fear can produce erratic and spontaneous behavior in both men and women. As men, we go through a lot to make our women happy. This rings true even if it means concealing that we, too, are scared. We all have something from the past we fear, but it must not supersede our faith. Over time, this will guide us into the future. In fact, it may be necessary to love the hell right out of him. That may be a little difficult, but for starters, you'll have to use your powers as a goddess to keep his energy focused.

In retrospect, men of modern society still must go out *hunting*. They must bring home the bacon for their family. This either means entrepreneurship or finding work outside the home. A paycheck represents power and respect. Instead of hauling a two-hundred-pound buffalo home, we do our best to bring home paychecks. Today, more women are bringing home the bacon than ever before (no pun intended). Dependent on the industry, women are out-earning their husbands, and with the recent downturn of the economy and children to take care of — all hands must be on deck! An influx of businesses owned by African-American women is on the horizon. Data shows an increase of 322% since 1997, making Black queens the fastest growing group of entrepreneurs in the United States![1]

In Will Durant's rare book, *The Oriental Heritage: The Story of Civilization*, he wrote: "Children were economic assets, and men gathered wives to draw children from them like interest. Wives and children were, in fact, the slaves of the man. The more a man had of them, the richer he was. Oddly, the poor man practiced monogamy, but he looked upon it as a shameful condition, from which some day he would raise to the position of a polygamous male."[2]

Can you imagine how broke men walked around with one wife while the dudes with the big bank had several wives cooking all kinds of gourmet meals? One can only picture the smile on their faces to have such a luxury of multiple wives and a pride of children.

Primitive men expected women to be useful and industrious. Women also expected this of themselves and their daughters. By the same token, boys were trained to provide and protect their family — by any means necessary. It was not so much about being fine, voluptuous, and beautiful. Yet, at the same time, these qualities were and still are appreciated most men. She was to be an economic asset rather than a liability. Women who are educated, spiritually religious, have sharp housekeeping and kitchen skills, and wear their own naturally grown hair are more valuable than women that fall short with any of these. She, too, has to value and take care of her natural body. This type of woman (in my own personal opinion) is worth her weight in a million diamonds and deep green emeralds.

Kings past and present understand the value of having a woman in their life. Life is much easier for those men that enjoy a woman by their side. We know a man could build something of significance with her wisdom guiding his energy in order to reach his heart's destiny. There are numerous examples of this in history: Nefertiti and Akhenaten of Kemet (ancient Egypt) built some wonderful edifices; the late Nelson Mandala and his wife Winnie Mandala; and President Barack Obama with his wife, First Lady Michelle Obama. It's vitally important for a man with vision to seek knowledge from great women who are truly happy with their lives. These women have accomplished a respectable level of success. Allow them to teach you how to reign as the all-around queen you are. The Queendom is in you! Take the time to learn how to improve your temperament, home cooking, interpersonal skills, and kindness. You shouldn't want to be a wife if you're not wife material. All it takes for most women is a slight tune-up and adjustment like an oil change, while it may take a whole engine rebuild for others. If you are equipped with these skills, a man will pay any price for you, even if it means sacrificing his empire. Is it even possible to place a price on a goddess? No, I think not.

DIVINE PRICE

Nowadays in civilized societies, men don't pay a dowry with gold, precious stones, cows, or sheep. We do pay a price by buying endless dinners, spending hours at the mall, talking on the phone, reading a million text messages, and listening to conversations that don't hold our interest at times. Chivalry is very much alive. Men just have a different approach to dating in modern society.

A decent dinner will cost $50 to $60. The average gentleman can't afford to pay that on a weekly basis and keep up with his bills and other responsibilities. He shouldn't feel pressured to do so. If he does, there is no way the relationship can be genuine, even though he wants to treat you like the most important woman in the world in his heart. Furthermore, you shouldn't be with a man who can't afford to invest quality time and energy into you.

If he has a realistic business idea in which he actively works on, he may just need some real support from you to get to the next level as his lady, his queen, and his motivation. You shouldn't feel obligated to believe in his dream, but if by chance you wholeheartedly do, then you should support him with all your will. Fan his little fire of dreams as if you had the Wings of Auset, the Kemetan Goddess! Turn his spark into a flame. You could be the difference between him failing or making it. Ultimately, this means you both have succeeded!

Just because he's a man, you don't have to yield everything to him. Test his spirit. There also need to be requirements met on his behalf. Don't throw him out of the picture because his financial status doesn't meet your standards. The money will eventually come. Judge him by what his actions manifest. Listen to his desires and read his energy. Take the time to evaluate the kind of energy he will bring into your world and the type of world the two of you will design together. The last thing you want is a man who operates on a low level of consciousness and is a chump.

Will he bring the love energy you've been praying for, or will he bring a curse to you?

Like positivity, the effects of negativity are limitless. It is critical to understand what type of energy this perfect guy is bringing to your doorstep. Ask yourself: "Is he bringing negative forces into my world, or a positive one? Blessings or curses? Unicorns or Gremlins?"

For instance: will he bring baby mama drama, have police constantly at your house, give you Black eyes, or deplete your life savings? The list can go on and on. Everything isn't going to be hunkydory. Make it your business that you have more positive aspects in your lives together.

Let's look at the flip side of the equation. He has a great relationship with his baby's mother that is on a purely platonic level for the sake of the kids, supports you, and he adds money to your bank account. The later scenario places you in a win-win situation, while the former example guarantees you heartache. Now, just as I have asked those questions about him, reverse the mirror on yourself. What kind of energy are you bringing to the table? Here's a better question: As a Mother God, what type of energy are you manifesting? You must make the choice in the world you create!

BALANCE

Marriage, for the most part, was socially accepted as a profitable partnership in which a woman and man worked together. They parented their children in a cooperative fashion. When a parent — in this case a single mother — provides food, clothes, and shelter for her children, she is supplying necessities. What we need are advanced levels of love and care for the home. This takes place when the feminine and masculine principles — known as the mother and father — work together to create the balance. They will be more prosperous by putting their energy together. This occurs more frequently than if they were to consistently work, pray, and plan alone. We are not meant to be alone, but that doesn't mean you are meant to settle.

ONE WITH NATURE

Through the intimate relationship with the plant world, women of the primordial period ascertained a wealth of knowledge.[3] A woman was the bread of life, the milk of renewed strength, and harvested the food crops that kept people fed and alive. Women were considered the "goddesses of agriculture." They had expertise in growing rice, corn, wheat, barley, tapioca, or any other crop to eat and sell. It's no wonder women were revered as Mother God, for she provided nourishment for the body. Everybody ate. I'm not saying the women of today don't have a lot of responsibilities, but the queens of the past understood the world. They would be headed backward without their power.

Since the beginning of civilization, women understood their spiritual power, which supersedes all power. However, they did not have as many distractions as the women of today: social media and television. You are stressed, overworked, exhausted, and starving for love, affection, intimacy, emotional guidance, and intimacy.

Let's elaborate on Auset, in order to further prove the importance of ancient women and their societal contributions. *Under his wings* originally came from Queen Auset, who imitates the pelicans and falcons and other mother birds along the Nile River. They kept their chicks under their wings for protection, care, and guidance. The Nile River is the longest river in the world (6,853 km long) and was the main source of food. It brought people from many parts of Africa, the motherland, together forming the greatest civilization ever known to the human race — Kemet. The Nile River and mothers share one thing in common: everyone depended on both to survive. The Mother Goddess, Queen Auset, took her man under her wing to protect the throne. She was also known as Queen of Heaven, Demeter, and, later, the Black Madonna. Flowers and fruits are among the typical symbols of the Great Mother Goddess.

You are there to protect your man's vision, which the Creator gave to him. The ancient Egyptian Queen Auset surrounded her husband with her "wings of Auset" to protect him. Queen Auset was also identified as the protector of the children, commoners, nobles, and the maternal protector of the ruling king. Notice how the wing covers him. She protects his heart, his vision, and his destiny.

YOUR PURPOSE EXERCISE

Below is an exercise to help you discover your purpose and, most importantly, assist you in focusing your energy to accomplish your goals:

1. Write down at least ten of your unique talents, abilities, gifts, and successes.

2. For each of your special qualities listed, write down the challenges each one brings to you.

3. Once you've finished, step away for five minutes and grab a drink of water.

4. Try not to talk or text anyone. Keep your focus on returning to the exercise.

5. Once you have your paper or journal in your hand, read it out loud. You don't have to shout, but your voice must be loud enough to hear yourself. Avoid mumbling.

BLACK WOMAN'S VALUE

Everyone wants to feel important and special. I find it hard to believe that anyone would love to be treated like crap, belittled, or ignored. Feeling good about yourself is an essential part of life. Self-confidence will help you control your emotions and make better decisions in your business life and personal life, especially when it comes to dating with the purpose of building a solid foundation with a man.

Unfortunately, too many foul (and sometimes evil) men take advantage of our young ladies because they were the first to tell them how beautiful they are and to tell them they "love'm." They are cheated on, they are victims of various types of abuse (mental, emotional, verbal, etc.), and they have to deal with financial infidelity.

Someone must take the time to teach our young ladies how special they are and educate them on their history. For instance, in Alkebulan, men honored African women as queens, Mother Gods, priestesses, empresses, and goddesses. It wasn't simply because of their sexy curves or the power from their sexual energy. It was because African women were held in the highest regard. Most people have heard of the "Valley of the Kings." Well, the "Valley of the Queens," located in Kemet, the Northeast region of Africa, was built to bury the wives of the pharaohs and is just as impressive. The Black woman was the first deity to be worshipped.[4] We are talking about eighteen thousand to one hundred thousand years ago.

Black women felt very good about themselves in the world.[5] There wasn't a drop of doubt in their confidence or sheer essence of feminine pulchritude. They were also well-protected and highly revered by the males, the defenders of the community. Men understood that their source of power and energy came from the woman. Additionally, African women were the first beauty queens of the world and inspired the imagination of human creative thought. This is evident in the female statues that can still be seen today throughout the world. There is nothing wrong with a little makeup, but there is no need to alter your face, hair, and body in the futile attempt to look like someone you are not. Women today should adorn themselves in their original glory.

For many chauvinistic males, it would be difficult to believe that women were on the thrones as sole rulers, but the fact remains that this was the way of life for advanced civilizations throughout Alkebulan and other parts of the world: Babylon (9 B.C.E.), Nigeria with Queen Aminia; Kemet (Ancient Egypt) with Queen Tye; Cush

(Kush) (Ethiopia) with Queen Makeda (Sheba); and other Nubian Queens, such as Queen Candace; and the Angolan Queen, the one and only Queen Nzinga.

Without the pleasure of the feminine gender, the world would self-destruct. Most men appreciate this fact on the physical level, but it's the energy that's generated through the love vibrations of the heart during sexual unity that makes the union a powerful one. With this unification, men and women can rule the world as equal partners in power and glory. Dr. Ivan Van Sertima, world historian and professor, stated in this legendary book, *Black Women of Antiquity*: *"Great Wives" of the pharaohs because of their role in the matrilineal succession assured them of tremendous prestige, enabling some to equal and even exceed their husbands in positions and power."* The main reason African women were viewed as subservient to men was because of the women-hating European church fathers of the third and fourth centuries.[3] They were sexually ambiguous, maladjusted, and — in many cases — openly homosexuals. They envied the female principle, especially one in authority. Similar to today's businesswomen, Kemet and Cush were filled with queens with their own sovereignty. We are taught in church that the trinity is comprised of the Father, the Son, and the Holy Ghost. The true and original trinity is the Mother, the Father, and the Child, which was Heru-ru (Haroeris). This is where the word *hero* comes from. Biologically speaking, a man cannot create a man or a woman. A woman can create both a girl and a boy. Women are blessed with the gift of creation.

The historical reality is that Europeans successfully circumvented the union between the most powerful union on earth, which is the Black woman and Black man. They accomplished this in Africa and on the fields of slave plantations of the colonies. The ramifications of this can be seen in today's American society. Pick up any newspaper, read an online news article, or watch the news. The degradation of Black women is evident within prominent cultures. The core of any family is love and respect, which is seriously lacking in our world today.

Dear Queen,

Your job is to bring his destiny into
fruition — speak blessings over him.
Hopefully he's doing the same.

CHAPTER 2

GODDESS

"A goddess is a female being believed to be the source of life and being and worshiped as a deity."

A female god or deity.
A greatly admired or adored woman.
A woman of great beauty.

*W*omen were highly revered, and it was a sacrilege to disrespect her. In fact, it was punishable by death. This high respect toward women in the ancient world projected Black women as queens of the universe and goddesses. The continuation of life was possible through the womb of a woman. Their status was so important that both men and women would kiss the ground they walked upon. The Ashanti tribe (located in central Ghana) is a perfect example. They believed that the bond between mother and child was the keystone of all social relationships.[1]

Furthermore, the role of the woman as the "sacred vessel" was expressed and depicted in multiple ways by the priests throughout many ancient cultures and high civilizations. Women were valued not just in tribal meetings, the kitchen, worship chambers, and bed-rooms — but also throughout the universal scheme of things. It was understood that a woman's womb is the creator of life. Their feminine energy was meant to inspire, encourage, and uplift people from the dead, whether in the literal sense or figuratively speaking. The first recorded resurrection was performed by a woman, Queen Auset of Kemet. This historical phenomenon was engraved on the pyramid walls of Kemet. The priests of the ancient high cultures kept precious holy pots and golden urns filled with water in their temples and sanctuaries to represent the ever-present reality of the feminine reproductive, resurrecting, and nurturing powers.[2]

With this sacred knowledge of the feminine energy, a loving, optimistic woman constantly strengthens and gives new life to her man and all those under her influence. Your spiritual prowess can resurrect any man from his deathbed of pity and regrets so that he believes in himself again. Your ability as a woman to pray and deeply encourage those for which you care about their successes should never be taken for granted. On the flip side of the coin, an antagonistic, negative, and pessimistic woman can destroy a man to the point in which he no longer believes in his dreams. A man raining on another man's parade has little to no effect on us in comparison to a woman's discouragement toward a man.

Let's reference the Bible to get a clearer understanding of the Mother God concept. This will give you an understanding of the power your words carry as a goddess. Proverbs 31:3 states: "Give not thy strength unto women, nor thy ways to that which destroyeth kings."

In other words, stay away from promiscuous women. Don't waste time with women that destroy the dreams of kings.

FOUR SEASONS

The love energy coming to and from couples should be reciprocal. A good king is looking for a queen who has an abundance of positive energy to replenish him. He desires a queen who makes him believe in himself, even when he stops believing in himself. Courting or dating someone for at least four seasons gives you a decent amount of time to test and measure a companion's level of love energy, consciousness, loyalty, faith, and consistency. The signs will be there to make a decent judgment of his character and energy level. Does he have electrifying "Star Power" energy or is his light dim? Is he a chump or a champion? Can you both carry your love and can it stand the ultimate test of time? You may meet a man at a great time in his life when everything is going smoothly. Yet, what happens if his life and your plans suddenly take a nosedive? He may suddenly lose his job months down the line. His energy might turn cold toward you and the world, and you may find yourselves in constant friction.

There is no way I can ever agree with marrying someone after only knowing them for a couple of days, weeks, or months. There are too many skeletons in some people's closet to go through in a short period of time. Sexually transmitted diseases and/or demons, too, can take time to reveal themselves. You should be concerned if the person you're going to marry has demons inside of them. It's better to discern that during the dating phase and not after you've jumped the broom. If the guy you're dating has a demon(s) in him, its mission is to destroy the goddess within you; to ensure that you won't be able to give birth to your purpose. The four seasons of a year should be sufficient to observe his spirit, test his will, and pray about him; however, it doesn't take long to measure the chemistry and energy between the two of you. Read the signs.

Relationships at their highest points are electrifying and rejuvenating. Their energy will have you coming back for more of that magnetic connection. Most marriages start off at a high voltage, and then at some point it becomes a struggle to maintain that same level of love energy. The good times diminish and misunderstandings increase. One reason this happens is because the couple stops uplifting each other. Take the time to edify your partner, and your partner will edify and love you. They will honor you in return, according to the simply law of correspondence. This states our current reality is a mirror of what is going on inside us.

It's one of the most beautiful laws of life.

THE EAGLE'S COURTSHIP –
PUT HIM TO THE TEST

A female eagle tests the male to challenge his commitment, strength, flight speed, dexterity, commitment, motion, and (my favorite) courage.[3] As a female, she is highly concerned about her safety and security. She wants to know if he will commit to taking care of her and their eaglet. When it comes time for a female eagle to choose her mate, she prepares herself for many potential partners. After carefully analyzing the one with the most potential, she picks him to fly with her for a while. If she likes his "flight swag," she finds a sizable stick and flies very high with it. At some point, she drops the stick to see if the male has grasped the vision and was paying enough attention to catch it.

She wants his undivided attention if he is going to get her treasure for life. If he does a great job of catching the stick, she will fly to an even greater height with a larger stick and drop it. She will continue to pick up larger sticks and fly even higher with each one. He continues to bring it back to her after he catches it every time.

The final part of this endurance test is picking up the heaviest piece of wood (the size of a small log) that she can fly with in her talons and gripping it with all her strength. She then drops it after flying as high as she can. Bald eagles can fly at a very high rate of speed, such as 65 mph. Their dives can reach the speed of 200 mph. This courtship is a sight to see! They are living out their love plane — the stronger the love is between the love birds, the further the two can go and have a lasting relationship.

If the male drops the stick, the female eagle flies away. This signifies he isn't worthy of her just yet. He'll be lucky to get a second chance because she is off to find the male she will crown as her king for life. The animal kingdom understands that their lineage is at stake, so they are conscious and discreet with whom they choose to mate.

Another test given by the female eagle is a free fall from a very high altitude. The masculine eagle will then fly to meet her in the air while she takes a dive. His job in this courtship is to lock talons with her before she hits the ground. If he doesn't, then she will meet her fate of death. This shows that he can protect her and will be committed to their family and in life's journey together as one. He can defend them from all dangers that a predator may bring to their world. When the male eagle passes all her tests, she crowns him as her king. Then, they proceed to build a nest/home together that can weigh up to a ton. Eagles are connected for life. They are in it to win it. They are each other's ride or die.

Far too many women crown men as their king because they love the façade that males portray. Some even fall in love with a man's social media profile and YouTube® videos. Take notes from the female eagles. Test his courage, patience, commitment, and righteous love for you. Never test him with an interrogation with hundreds of questions. That can get annoying and scare him away. Actions are louder than words and speak for themselves. Test and watch him like the eagle.

Nevertheless, testing a man by throwing sticks won't help you much, but asking yourself the following questions before investing your divine energy will help you in the long run remarkably:

1) Will this man fight to protect you and your honor?

2) Is he dependent on his mother to handle problems?

3) Will he put his career, money, and material possessions before you?

4) Does he possess the patience to wait for your sweet, life-giving, heaven-on-earth treasure?

5) Is he committed to seeing you succeed in life and creating a successful relationship together?

6) Does he express the right kind of love energy for you?

7) Is it a righteous love? A healthy love that shows he wants you to grow, advance, and excel in life?

8) Will he be able to love the children you've given birth to with another man?

9) Can he become a great father to your children?

10) Does he honor his word?

A righteous love has no strings attached. It's the type of love that uplifts both the persons giving and receiving it. It is a love that wants you to grow, sing, shine, prosper, and advance. Just because someone says they love you, it doesn't mean they have your best interests in mind. What one says and does are two completely different realities. A real man will not only make you feel safe, but he will show you he can handle and embrace your position as a goddess.

REBUILDING OUR KINGS

As mentioned in the previous chapter, the first historically known resurrection was not by a male as we have been taught for generations. Instead, it was performed by Queen Anset in Kemet. [4] Her faith and passionate energy to will her man back to life awakened her husband, Ausar, from the dead. The Kemetic story starts with Ausar being butchered into pieces by Set, his jealous brother. Nevertheless, Queen Auset was determined to find all his body parts. She focused her energy on putting her man back together. Imagine what would happen if every woman focused on rebuilding one broken man.

If, and only if, men are going to take their natural leadership role as a provider and protector, it's going to take true queens to encourage us to be the best men we can be! It's going to take your love, energy, passion, and natural tenderness to awaken the greatness out of us. Queen Auset's energy was so powerful that she transformed into a falcon and flapped her wings over Ausar's body until the fresh wind blew air into his body. The wind brought his spirit back into the physical world.[5]

This was the original Immaculate Conception that our African ancestors left on the pyramid walls of ancient Egypt. The story of Mary is based from the story of Auset. Joseph, Mary's husband, was originally Ausar. Through this worship session a special child was conceived, their son, Heru-ru (Hero), which represents Jesus. Heru-ru's bravery was used to fight and defeat his uncle Set. [This is where the word hero was born.] A strong father and an energy force from the mother create the most beautiful miracle — a child.] This is the foundation of human life — a female and a male procreating.

"Beside every great man there is an outstanding woman."

At times, it will take a woman, the queen, the Mother Goddess, to cook up a recipe of love and encouragement to keep her man awakened. It's the feminine energy force that motivates and stimulates the human intellect. This is relevant in men as well. I have often heard people say: "behind every great man there is a great woman." I believe it's "beside every great man there is an outstanding woman." This statement is true and has always been the case since the beginning of time. There are plenty of statues that were built in Kemet with couples standing next to each other. Our African ancestors left us clues and it's about time we take them seriously. Obviously, whatever we are doing now to build and maintain our families isn't working.

Make it a top priority to reach a higher level of consciousness as a couple. Both of you can tap into the powers of God and divine intelligence. Some people call it the Holy Ghost or God consciousness. Allow the spiritual aspects of life to have a prevalent role in your world. If you're single, that's okay. This book was written with you in mind. Focus your creative energy on building a lasting empire of love and generosity that will last for generations long after you're gone. All you should do is put your mind, energy, and consciousness toward accomplishing this goal of spiritual enlightenment.

A WOMAN'S WORLD

Barbara G. Walker, scholar and author of *Woman's Encyclopedia of Myths and Secrets*, made a powerful statement regarding the magnitude of women:[6]

"Because birds travel freely between the earthly and heavenly realms, they were regarded as angelic messengers — givers of omens, possessors of the occult secrets, and soul carriers. Carrion crows and vultures took souls to heaven. Storks brought them back to Earth for rebirth. Wise owls told the secrets of the night. Lustful doves and nightingales told the secrets of love. Angelic eagles foretold the future."[6]

That is why Queen Auset transformed into a bird. She flew into the spiritual plane carrying Ausar's spirit back into the physical. Pay attention to what this signifies. Whether we believe this anecdote or not, it's extremely powerful! The ancient Kushites (Ethiopians) and Kemetians (original Black Egyptians) believed it was possible to take something real from your mind and pull it from a thought to make it tangible. Anyone who exercises faith believes in this concept too. In fact, I believe it wholeheartedly. Their prayers, positive energy, consciousness, solid relationships, and meditations made their ancient civilizations extremely successful and powerful. There is nothing impossible for those with faith in God and those who remain steadfast with their vision. Their consciousness of who they were and what was possible knew no boundaries. Walking around knowing that you are a little god, or a goddess, says a lot! Now that's the type of revelation that will turn your life around!

Today, we live in a male-dominated and patriarchal society where women are subjected to consistently making themselves look more attractive. They do this to catch a man. Aren't you tired of catching a man? It's time for your king to find you. It's time to place more emphasis on spiritual matters. These aspects about yourself will improve your inner beauty, which will be a blessing to all those around you. They will last a lifetime.

Patriarchal societies prefer for women to be unnatural, unsuccessful, uneducated, undefended, and unresisting. Naked, barefoot, in the kitchen, and bearing their children. Women must represent all of this, while at the same time, they must always maintain their stunning beauty. Almost every major modern-day industry is male-dominated: the car industry, satellite broadband, and the technology industry. Contrary to popular belief, many societies in ancient Africa operated in female-dominated matriarchal societies for thousands of years. In retrospect, women were the prominent rulers. Western Asian, Arabic, and European women were astonished by the freedom, intellect, and power African women held in their matriarchal societies. The successions went from mother to daughter; the male companion entered the family of his wife. Women were the "Queen Mothers of the Universe," "The Givers of Life," and "Mother Gods." They were protected for thousands of years before the Father God concept was planted in the motherland through the colonization of the Europeans. Notice how every time of which God is spoken, the Creator is referred to as a male [him, his, and my father in Heaven] in churches, schools, and the streets?

Nonetheless, one might wonder about the men's whereabouts during this time period. The warrior kings were inspired to provide for and protect their family and the village. Taking on his responsibility gave the process of manifestation an opportunity: great ideas into reality through the spiritual energy and power of his queen. Women and men were coregents of the given kingdom. Everyone was not a queen or king; however, everyone had a sense of responsibility, self-love, and respect for their communities. This allowed them to have a level of trust, which increased the support system within the families, communities, and governments. The social system was intact, and it was all based on the foundation of honoring the women, whom are the givers of life.

"A woman is the flower in the garden, and the man's job is to protect that garden by any righteous means necessary."

Females ignited the creative energies in the men of their communities, which generated the ideas that manifested in all the wonderful monuments, sculptures, pyramids, and inventions. Queens encouraged their "warrior kings" to defeat the odds in momentous battles and to reach higher toward their dreams in both the spiritual and physical dimensions of life. There are no boundaries to what can manifest for couples with a high level of faith. The result is one woman and one man whom are both like-minded individuals, merging their two worlds together. Women and men once ruled their world side by side in their respective roles, hand in hand in unison. There were no power struggles over who had control over the kingdom. Both knew their intricate roles in the grand scheme of things.

"You're the Queen of the universe and he's the King. Why are you fighting over superiority? You're both royalty!" Dr. Ishakamusa Barashango

Dear Queen,

Women have been proven to be a key resource in uplifting men's spirits and confidence. For thousands of years, men believed women possessed magical powers and divine wisdom. For these two reasons, amongst many others, women were highly honored in society and enhanced societies throughout many civilizations in the ancient world, especially in Africa. History is known to repeat itself. What happened before can happen again, right here and right now!

CHAPTER 3

COOKING QUEEN

Cooking is therapeutic and has magical powers!

*D*uring a trip to the grocery store with a female acquaintance, I bumped into one of my favorite high school teachers in the vegetable aisle. I hadn't seen Ms. Hall since I graduated in 1999. After we hugged, I asked her if she still taught home economics.

"Not anymore, Kevin," she said. "I retired back in 2001 so I could enjoy my life. I feel bad sometimes about leaving because these women today don't know how to cook or sew. Nor are they efficient at taking care of their home. The sad part is that nobody is teaching them. They can't know if they aren't being taught like when the Home Economics course was mandated in school in the 1990s. Many schools removed Home Economics out of the curriculum. The school boards didn't see it as important."

Before we parted ways, she told me, "I hope you find a woman who loves to cook."

Ms. Hall still understood the importance and benefits of a home-cooked meal. She valued the tradition. There is no substitution for a meal prepared at home. The home is where you can cry, laugh, heal, and remain in solitude for as long as you would like. It's a place of worship, lovemaking, and peacefulness. It is a place you can eat deliciously prepared meals. Food sustains life. Food is medicine. You can heal almost any illness through the type of foods you serve. Therefore, ladies, home cooking is power!

Food is composed of important nutrients: minerals, vitamins, carbohydrates, and proteins — all of which provide energy that allows us to function efficiently. Your family is your nation and kingdom. Protect it by any righteous means necessary from invading forces, i.e., diseases. Preparing healthy meals, such as greens, will do wonders to the body. Whatever is fed to the body is fed to the brain. Wouldn't you rather feed your brain fuel to help keep the positive energy flowing? There are foods that do the exact opposite to our bodies.

Many times, we bring the enemy right through the front door of our home with a smile on our faces. This is the food that gives us high blood pressure, cancer, and tumors in various parts of our body. Everyone in the house is going to follow your lead because you are their Mother God. As a matter of fact, "house" means *mother* throughout the continent of Africa. The village homes represent unique, circular architectural designs, which symbolize an extension of the mother's womb. Queen Afua — an internationally recognized holistic health practitioner, author, and womb wellness coach — is one the biggest Cooking Queens alive! Her cooking instructions begin with advising people to become conscious of whether they are feeding their families with low or high vibrational foods. A high vibrational diet consists of foods that are ALIVE (i.e., organic fruits and vegetables) and that positively benefit the person, as well as the planet. She advises us to rethink the way in which we look at the kitchen, rather than by viewing it as the "Healing Laboratory."[1] The formulas (prepared meals) we create can either heal the household or diminish the health of the very same people we love and vow to protect.

When you take the time to cook in a world where no one has time to stand in the kitchen for more than twenty minutes, a man will automatically know that you will bring some level of peace into his life. It's hard for anyone to remain happy when they're always hungry. Their stomachs will constantly growl and sound like a motorcycle. There is nothing soothing about starving. Eating healthy meals helps a woman, man, and child [trinity] to think clearly and calmly. This, in turn, allows us to make wise decisions.

As Queen Mother, you are in control of how the family functions. The vibrant Queen Mother Shahrazad Ali once said the following in a relationship lecture:

"How long our men are going to live, and under what condition he is going to be in, is determined by the cooking of women. The hands of the nation are in your hands as a woman. That is an enormous amount of power, and should not be taken lightly."[1] At the same time, a man should be independent and not dependent on a woman for meals or anything else.

She is right, when you think about it. We can control how healthy our families are eating at the dinner table. By doing so, you're giving your children and husband/king a fighting chance of being able to think clearly. They are able to live a healthier lifestyle, which may increase their lifespan. Likewise, they are able to go out into the world with the necessary energy to conquer it. Isn't that the whole point? Isn't the point to see and love on those that you love and hold closest to you for as long as possible? (You can even determine how good the sex is going to be in your marriage through the types of food you prepare in your kitchen "healing laboratory." Is he going to be a Mr. Long Ranger or Sir Quick Stop? Healthy foods also help and inspire men's lovemaking to reach a higher level. Sounds like an incentive to me!

There is no place like home. If you believe this to be true, then you know there is no substitution for a home-cooked meal. Have you ever had a meal that tastes so good that it's memorable? It has the power to make you slap yourself or bite your tongue. This food leaves us with the natural expression *mmm-mmm*-gooood feeling after the meal is complete. Well, you can cook more than food. You can cook up a bright future based on the ingredients you use in your life.

HEALTHY LIVING VS. FAST FOOD

Historically, women harvested food planted in the earth, brought it home, and cooked it. This created a meal that sustained life and increased the advancement of civilizations. In America today, many career women depend on fast-food restaurants to bring home food to feed their families, while others take sack lunches. I've heard this phrase time over again: *People don't have time to cook anymore.* Fellas must keep their fingers crossed when asking a woman if she cooks.

Building a strong empire with healthy food is not only a great idea, but it's necessary for survival. In other words, build your family to thrive with the healthy meals you prepare. When it comes down to it, we should be eating to live long, not living to eat and die sooner rather than later. Some of the foods we eat are eating us alive, such as: fried chicken, ice cream, pizza, white flour, and sugar. Fried foods are non-digestible, constipating, and remain in the body. This causes flabby skin, a large gut, digestion issues, heartburns, gas, and unhealthy chemical reactions to the brain. The combination of foods with edible drugs — such as preservatives, additives, and dyes — results in behavior control and chemical warfare upon the health.[2] Seventy million people in the United States suffer from digestive disorders such as acid reflux, diarrhea, and gastroesophageal reflux disease (GERD).[3] Over time, the results of generational unhealthy eating habits are detrimental to our families and community. The recipes that were passed down to us, and the ones we pass down to our children, are either generational blessings or generational curses.

White sugar, which is processed, robs us of our body's minerals and vitamins, especially Vitamin E. Dr. Llaila O. Afrika, states: "These ingredients result in drowsiness, diabetes, oxygen-starved brain, temper outbursts, hyperactivity, mood swings, kidney failure, tantrums, mischievousness, delinquency, laziness, and violence. A simple change in our diets will create miracles."[2]

There are two reasons I'm telling you this in a relationship book:

1) It's better to have a relationship with two healthy and happy individuals.

2) Some traditional hardworking men may anticipate their wives or the woman of the house to have dinner ready when they get home.

You may not like it, Millennial ladies, but too many men think it's a deal-breaker to have a woman who doesn't cater to him. In the same respect, wouldn't you want your man to have dinner prepared for you when you get home? Men should be able to cook as well. The duty of preparing dinner, lunch, and breakfast should be shared to some degree. The best cook in the home, however, should do a majority of the cooking. This is regardless of gender. Let the best cook work their magic! Figure out the winning formula that works best for your family to grow together.

If you are a woman who still believes in taking care of home, I encourage you to answer the following questions:

1. Does the food you prepare contain good fuel for your body?

2. Can people feel the love of God in the energy projected in your food?

3. Do you take time to pray over your meals as a family at the dinner table?

If you answered yes to only one of these questions or none of the above, it's time to conduct a self-evaluation about your time in the kitchen. If your answer is yes to all three of these questions, whomever you choose to crown is one lucky son of a queen!

THE SYMBOLISM BEHIND THE DINNER TABLE

The dinner table represents a circle of energy, which can be either negative or positive. It's a place for prayer, fellowship, and exchanging love energy. "Food for the soul" can be a great meal, a good book, or an exhilarating conversation. It's also anything that makes you feel awesome deep down inside your soul. It gives you a sense of accomplishment meant for you and your well-being. The gratification is like enjoying your favorite song, talking with a best friend, or going to your favorite place. The pleasure of feeding our soul reaches the hidden parts of our brain, heart, and body. Soul food can make you feel that good. Everything is so fast-paced today that we are conditioned to eat. We can't satisfy our nutritional needs without taking time to feed our soul.

In the beginning of relationships, we're so concerned about what we bring to the table. This may be concerns such as: accolades, resumes, Bible scriptures, and investment portfolios. Try bringing an actual nutritious and delicious meal. Delicious home-cooked meals can make you feel like you're blessed. Cooking is an art form that transforms an average-looking woman into a dime piece — a winner!

We're taught that food is a way to a man's heart, but if you haven't figured it out yet — it's also a way to a man's wallet. Before direct deposit became available, men would hop all the way home from work. They happily gave their paychecks directly to their wife with no hesitation. And why not? His wife took care of the house, cooked several times a week, and looked after the children. To top it off, many women today are bringing home their own paychecks. This adds to their family's financial security.

Now, I don't know about you, but I haven't heard of a man giving his wife his entire paycheck since the 1990s. This was a common practice in many two-parent homes. However, I've heard of women giving their whole paycheck to their man. The roles have been reversed. Could it be because women stopped cooking like they used to in the past? Or is it because men stopped working to take care of the home and are mainly working for themselves?

A man must feel like he's needed and wanted. There should be room for him at the table, even if he's making less money than you are. A man of quality must know that you will take care of your children together. Furthermore, he wants to be assured that his ego and stomach will be well-nourished. This is confirmation whether or not he is in for the long haul. Of course, there is a lot more to men than that. It gives you a great chance in cultivating a special relationship. It is my hope that this special relationship leads to a walk down the aisle.

The dinner table represents the common rituals of eating, praying, and conversing. Without this ritual, the dinner table will collect dust as well. I love traditions because they remind us of our history. They help us keep our culture alive. The recipes our parents passed down to us were also passed down to them. Cooking isn't old school or out of style, but that's the impression many Millennial women believe for some reason.

Several months before publishing this book, it was featured for a dating segment at the South Florida Book Festival. A woman in the crowd, which consisted of sixteen women and four men, admitted she didn't have the time to cook for herself. Not to mention, she lacked the time to sufficiently cook and eat with her man. Another young lady stated that cooking was old school. She emphasized that it was all about drive-thru or TGIF pickup. Ladies, when this is your perception of cooking, it could cause you to forfeit some of your power. The opportunity to have a great, traditional family man to court you is slipping away from you.

Let's get back to the basics and return to the dinner table. Moreover, let's get our families back in order!

REAL TALK. REAL FOOD.

In today's world, we are caught up in the rat race of job hunting and paying bills. Many believe they must keep up with the Joneses, along with celebrity breakups and makeups. All of this happens during the hustle and bustle of making ends meet. Having children doesn't make it any easier, especially for single mothers and fathers. Yet, I think children make life worth living. There are so many fast-food restaurants with quick, greasy meals. Both of these are costing consumers their lives and more money than they can afford to pay. There are 50,000 fast-food chains in America. There's an astonishing 500,000 fast-food chains around the world.[4] Finding an ambitious woman who has a great relationship with God and loves cooking in the kitchen is like winning the lottery. By preparing meals, you'll stand out like diamonds underneath the rays of the sun.

The average upright man who grew up with a loving mother, or mother figure, will desire to be with a queen who reflects his mother's love energy. This is especially accurate when it comes to dinner. A woman cannot ever replace a benevolent mother's love, but there is nothing wrong with doing your best to fan him with your love. You will represent the feminine principle that has nurtured, inspired, empowered, cooked, cleaned, and raised him to become the best man to his ability. Your job as his queen is to take the baton. Raise the standards and build him into the best king he can be!

Many of us, both male and female, experienced the miracles our mothers and/or grandmothers created when making meals in the kitchen. They completed this without money or enough food in the refrigerator. My siblings and I experienced this frequently with our mother. I remember sharing similar stories with our childhood friends. Our Queen-Mothers created meals from scratch. We often witnessed this phenomenon during holiday dinners and during rough times. Queen Rosette, my mom, made many miracles happen in her lifetime for her children and for the community. There is nothing like a person's smile after a good meal on an empty stomach.

This explains why quality men constantly look for the reflection of the love energy of the feminine principle, usually given by their mother and/or grandmother. We desire to experience those miracles as often as possible. A good man will look for you locally, but a great man will search the Seven Seas to find you. If he believes you're his dream woman, then you are the one who will unlock his destiny. You are the answer to his prayers. Kings will go the distance because our experience tells us that this kind of woman is extremely rare. In fact, these women only come around once in a lifetime.

Many of us who love to eat home-cooked meals may come from a traditional family. We pray that God will give us a fine-cooking queen who will continue the bloodline. If there is a hint of your scent out there in the world, he'll do whatever it takes to exchange energy with you, especially if he believes that his mother will approve of you. In the same respect, a man will love you. He will accept you as his wife, regardless of your cooking skills. True love conquers all.

COOKING UP A MILLION

Cooking is a form of creation. It's a form of lovemaking and gives us a chance to be creative. It's therapeutic and can be darn right lucrative. Pattie Labelle sold one pie every 72 seconds in one weekend alone. She cannot only sing her heart out, but her sweet potato pies also soothe the soul. She made more than 2.3 million dollars in a single weekend during November 2015. See, ladies, you don't have to pay a man with your cookies and milk. Cooking pays, and in Ms. Labelle's case it paid off big time.

Look at what other women are bringing to the dinner table; we're not just talking about food here. Cooking involves putting ingredients together and allowing them to marinate. Just like in business: if you place the right idea — at the right time — then you'll be able to cook a million.

It is my belief that more women will embrace the goddess within them with the help of a mentor to guide their energy. Connect with an older woman at your church, job, or neighborhood to show you the ropes in the home, marriage, and the kitchen. Even if you know how to cook well, there is always something new to learn. A true queen steps in to push others into their greatness. She assists others while helping them to fulfill their purpose in life. Everyone gets better around you. Males pull from this energy to gain strength to take on the world. Through women, men become kings. A man will continue to be a chicken, should you feed him like a chicken. Feed him like an eagle, and he'll soar!

DINNER GUEST: FIRST LADY MICHELLE OBAMA

Let's turn the spotlight on the dinner guest at the table: the beautiful 44th First Lady of the United States — Michelle Obama. One of her greatest talents is the ability to multitask. Once she went on an executive director interview with Sasha when Sasha was an infant because she couldn't find a babysitter. She got the job. She believes creating order in her home produces balance in her life, which we all know is filled with highs and lows.[5] She used the old school way (the best way, in my opinion) and sat down with a pen and paper. Michelle's process is to prioritize by writing out what needs to be done. Many guys are horrible at planning things, so an attentive woman who can come in and bring order into their life is a blessing. The First Lady is the wife to President Barack Obama. She is the mother of two beautiful girls, Malia and Sasha. She loves to cook big old-fashioned meals with a healthy twist.

Mrs. Obama was prepared to do whatever it took to push her family and the country forward. The United States has never seen a First Lady as involved on the grassroots level as the likes of Mrs. Obama. She's a far from average phenomenal woman prepared to raise the bar of excellence in any challenge.

"I come to this with many talents," she stated during an interview with the Associated Press on May 27, 2007. "I need to be prepared to do what the country needs me to do at the time. Whether that's baking cookies or serving as a wonderful hostess, that's my job. I have to be prepared to do what's necessary."[6]

She didn't come into her marriage, or the White House, with preconceived ideas of what to do in her new position. She just knew she was ready to do her best at whatever her role called for her king. The ability to make it happen is a key point and vital aspect that is to be loved and revered of strong women!

What's most interesting to me about Mrs. Obama is that she's health conscious. She's not only physically attractive, but her cooking is off the charts too! She initiated the *Let's Move!* fitness campaign for kids to tackle the childhood obesity epidemic in 2012. *Let's Move!* strives to get the entire community actively involved. It promotes a healthy lifestyle and fun physical activities, including being active in school and at home with the family.

Before Michelle LaVaughn Robinson became 44th First Lady of the United States, she was a graduate of Harvard Law School and Princeton University (graduating cum laude in 1985 with a B.A. in Sociology). As an attorney, she worked at a Chicago firm and held a city administrator position in Chicago as assistant to Mayor Richard Daley. Shortly after, she became assistant commissioner of planning and development for the city of Chicago, one of the largest cities in the United States. She understands politics, health, family, and how to support her man — President Barack Obama.

On top of her *Let's Move!* movement she was the force behind influencing chain restaurants, movie theaters, and take-out pizzerias to list calories on their menus. Like a true queen, she's serious about improving the health of children in America. The school lunch program feeds more than 21 million low-income children. It now requires school districts to serve more fruits, vegetables, lean protein, whole grains, and low-fat dairy products within their meals.

Mrs. Obama's relationship with healthy food started during her childhood on the South Side of Chicago. Fraser Robinson, her father, sold produce off the back of his vegetable truck as a boy. Her mother, Marian Robinson, helped care for a family plot in the neighborhood's World War II victory garden. These memories of her health-conscious parents were inspirations for the White House kitchen garden.[7] She understood the importance of feeding and eating from Mother Earth at an early age.

Her love for gardening, along with her law expertise and cooking background, places her at the top of the list as a Cooking Queen. There are so many great things about her. I think women should strive to emulate her qualities in some aspect of their life, regardless of political-social affiliation or culture. Michelle Obama is a phenomenal woman without a doubt!

PAVING THE WAY

Food has played a vital role during every era since civilization began. Women began developing a relationship with the earth by planting and gardening. Most of the foods, if not all, were organic and planted and eaten by those who grew it. Women took the time to plant and cook everything the family enjoyed. Historically, women harvested food planted in the earth, brought it home, and cooked it. This, in turn, created a meal that sustained life and increased the advancement of civilizations — hence the terms "Mother God," "Mother Earth," and "Mother Nature."

In today's fast-food society, most people eat in a living room instead of with their loved ones around a dining room table, even when there is a house filled with people. The microwave gets more usage and action than the stove. Fast-food restaurants profited nearly 191 billion dollars in 2013, while they are estimated to make 210 billion dollars by 2018.[8]

Man's early inventions, for the most part, have been created because he wanted to make his stomach happy. Food is a motivator! Therefore, primitive men hunted from sun-up to sun-down, placing their lives on the line. Consequently, many of them lost their lives. Even so, the invention of agriculture by women, paved the way from the semi-nomadic hunter-gatherer stage to the more relaxed, scientific investigative exploration stage. Women's ability to create a newer and safer way to eat, in comparison to hunting large and dangerous animals, allowed men to take less life-threatening chances in the wild, commencing the praise of women in Africa. The woman invented cooking to feed her child, herself, and her man. We are what we eat, and it is solely my belief that women knew this. Therefore, they promoted eating vegetables from the earth they cultivated and cooked.

In the earlier stages of human life, gathering plants, roots, and tubers to cook were amongst the daily tasks of women. These duties were tantamount to hunting and protecting the community, both of which were the role of the men. Due to the nature of hunting and war, the life of the male was limited. The level of violence and danger to bring food home to the family for survival was consistently high. Consequently, the death rate of men was — and still is — higher than that of women thousands of years later.

However, males directly earned respect for playing their role as providers and protectors. The females earned the respect of their male counterparts through caring, nurturing, and cooking. Taking care of family is the primary responsibility of both women and men. Once we get back to our traditional roles as a community, we will have a legitimate way of getting society back to our right minds. This can only happen if we uplift men as the natural protectors to guard them. This becomes crucial, so that they can uplift the women back to the position of power on the throne.

The African women of antiquity were the first in the world to plant crops, breed animals, make pots, spin, and weave — amongst other things. Becoming the first agriculturalists of the world is what women brought to the table. The art historian and author, Queen Mother Rosalind Jefferies, reminds us that the uncanny relationship between women of ancient times (and their plants and animals) was unprecedented.

Mrs. Jefferies states, "As the Primal Mother Creator, with fertilizing and nurturing powers extended from the firmaments down into the earth. Hence, this is the origin of the term 'Mother Nature.' A woman's powers of fertility in the universe were not limited to people, but could be magnified to affect vegetation, animal husbandry, and the atmosphere. Women were, and continue to be the 'Giver of Life'."[9]

THE QUALITIES OF A COOKING QUEEN:

1. She knows how to pick ripe fruits and vegetables by picking them in their peak season.

2. She prepares the ingredients for dinner the night before to save time.

    -   Seasons the food hours or a day in advance.

    -   Chops up the onions.

3. She uses discernment on what to cook, based on the health of her family.

    -   Understands the allergies of her family.

-   Serves high vibrational foods (fresh, certified organic fruits and vegetables), fresh squeezed juice, dried fruits, brown rice, whole-wheat macaroni, and vegetables.

4. She is patient with the foods she creates.

    -   Sets aside the time to cook.

    -   Not always in a rush to prepare a meal.

5. Her main ingredient in dishes is love.

    -   There are many ingredients that go into a dish, but when love is involved — it takes your meals to a whole new level.

6. Her food isn't just filling, but it also provides nourishment.

    -   The quality of the ingredients in the meals will give your guests energy or make them sluggish.

    -   You purposely seek out foods that contain high levels of nutrients and vitamins.

7. She offers dinner to the neighbors and her guests.

    -   Extends love by offering a meal to neighbors, friends, and co-workers.

8. She is creative with her dishes.

    -   Cooking dinner is an art form.

    -   Gets creative and tries different meal combination.

9. She seeks to please her family and friends.

    -   Feeding your family is one thing, but feeding them with the purpose of nourishing their souls makes your cooking excellent.

10. She teaches someone else how to cook.

- Invites children and relatives in the kitchen to pass down the recipes.

- Finds a young woman to mentor and shows her the ropes in the kitchen and around the home.

EXTENSION OF LOVE

Cooking can be an intimate and personal engagement. It's a way to make love to your significant other and a great way to be romantic. Eating a good meal as a family allows you to pray, enjoy fellowship, and generate positive energy together as a family unit. This gives you a feel for what is going on with your loved ones, while uplifting your spirits.

Imagine that the food being cooked originates from living organisms: plants and animals. Both are living species with energy, which is transferred into your body to give you sustenance. A car can't move without its battery, which acts as its energy source. The same thing goes with a family. The proper energy source will be healthy food and the righteous love, flowing from your hands into your family's soul. This creates "soul food." We need all the love energy that we can collect in this world. You have a chance to share your love in the way you prepare the food and serve it.

COOK WITH CAUTION

I am not suggesting that you cook for every man that arrives at your place. Not at all. Some women think they are showing themselves worthy by cooking their men food, washing his clothes, and even paying his bills. This takes place all while the woman is dating the man. All three of these are no-nos. You're proving yourself worthy in the wrong way. Show him you're a woman worthy of every dollar in his bank account. Talk about your own cooking. Converse about washing clothing or your methods toward keeping a clean house, both of which you paid for with your own money. Mention a couple business ideas. Then, at the right time, prepare an off-the-chain mouthwatering, jaw-dropping, make you say mmm-mmm good type of meal for him. Invite him to dinner and show him how regal you can be. Men are visual creatures, so he'll be able to see that you're a woman of quality that shouldn't be overlooked.

Cooking is an extension of your love toward your family, counterpart, and who you are as a full-fledged woman. In many countries — from long ago to now — preparing meals was ceremonial for the community. This is especially relevant during times of celebration, such as weddings, victory dinners after a war, and paying homage to the deceased ancestors. The women of the African villages spent days preparing meals. They viewed cooking as both a privilege and an honor. Many of these cooking ceremonies and traditions are still practiced today. We cannot afford to let these ancient traditions go because we'll lose part of our history and identity.

Cooking is therapeutic and a way to outwardly express your love. It takes time, patience, and, my favorite, creativity. Women can maintain their family and culture by cooking nutritious meals. Food has healing and medicinal powers. The ultimate hospital is the home.

Your grace in the kitchen will soothe your king's soul and calm his spirit. This, in turn, will give him the necessary energy to protect you and the family. You're managing the wellness, stability, and power of your family. That's a lot of power.

We need to bring the love back in our homes — starting in the kitchen!

Dear Queen,

Your home is your nation. Protect it by any means necessary from invading forces. Preparing healthy meals, which means a lot of greens, will work wonders for the body, mind, and soul.

CHAPTER 4

SPIRITUAL QUEEN

A Cherokee Proverb:

*A woman's highest calling is to lead a man
to his destiny. A man's highest calling
is to protect his woman, so that she can
roam the earth as free as a bird.*

omen have always been related to the bird because it was believed that they could fly into heaven and back into earth. In other words, women represented angels throughout the world. The significance of bringing what is in the spiritual world of heaven into the physical dimension gives you an unbelievable amount of power.

Every spiritual man wants to have a woman who will pray for him and with him. Incorporating faith makes the relationship a lot more enticing and interesting. For example, a husband and wife in Ancient Egypt went into a room, lit up incense, and meditated before they proceeded to pray to God to bless their union. They also offered up prayers for wisdom and strategy, as well as prayers of gratitude. They wanted to show their thankfulness for life. After they finished praying, they proceeded to make love, which intertwined their spirits deeper. This kind of lovemaking was the most powerful intercourse in which two people, or and two loving spirits, could ever engage in. This ancient tradition, known as maithuna, caused both parties to transcend into the highest level of consciousness — God consciousness.

Studying the master teacher, Dr. Ishakamusa Barashango, for several years opened my mind to the sacred love ceremony of maithuna. It gave our ancestors the ability to communicate with angels and tap into the supernatural. That's deep! I literally saw stars once while making love to my high school sweetheart as a teenager. I don't know how or why the stars appeared in my room that night, but there was something out of the ordinary that occurred during that space and time. The young lady also cried during her orgasm. It freaked me out, so we completely stopped. I held her in my arms for the rest of the night.

Due to the knowledge I've ascertained over the years, I am convinced that we communicated with angels that night. The equation was conducive for an out-of-this-world experience: love energy, intense passion, and dynamic chemistry between us! To this day I have yet to experience that level of ecstasy.

It would be impossible to make love with someone in this manner unless you were highly invested in each other's well-being: mind, body, and spirit. A woman has the power to harness her energy into something that can be fruitful or destitute, but she will give it her all. When you're connected with the right man – WATCH OUT, WORLD! Who knows what problems you and your king would be able to solve? The world is yours!

A PRAYING WOMAN

Imagine holding hands with your mate while running for your life at the top of a twenty-story building. At some point, you must take a leap of faith to successfully jump from one building to the next. The both of you will have to fight equally to maintain the relationship, which is so much easier and stronger. When you both agree on the high dimension of purpose for your union, you come together because you complement each other. Something magnificent will be created. A supernatural phenomenon. Go into marriage with a higher purpose other than financial stability, endless dinners, a sex buddy, and movies. Becoming more aware of the spiritual aspect of the relationship will give your marriage more hope than those couples who don't have the essential spiritual component.

Declare that . . .

> "We are coming together because something
> much greater is coming out of us!"

If a male doesn't want to jump in faith to accomplish things or to manifest your goals as a couple, the one who jumped first will make the leap and fall. In retrospect, the other lets go of your hand to watch the outcome. He will either get motivated to make the jump after seeing you were successful, or he will get discouraged after seeing you fall to your demise. The ideal situation is to jump together in confidence so that you will be successful in your journey together. This will eventually become your way of thinking and your way of life.

Prayer activates the powers of your prophetic spirit. Women are naturally in tune with their spirit, until some evil spirit(s) dims their light. As previously mentioned, there's a belief that women are connected to heaven due to their gentleness and association with Mother Nature. It is out of a woman's womb that we are born. A praying woman can pick up the vibrations of the cosmos, which will allow her to dress her children/family appropriately before stepping out into the public. The children are shielded by the angels of heaven before walking out the door into the world because their parents prayed over them. For this reason, a spiritual man will desire and seek out a praying woman in which to build a life. A woman worships the Creator because she comprehends that she will protect her royal bloodline through the power of prayer. Ninety percent of what happens in life occurs first in the spiritual dimension, also known as the unseen world. Praying allows you to elevate beyond the physical world. It gives us the ability to touch, see, feel, smell, and taste our physical existence. It's better to pray before you get into a dire situation. It's common for people to foresee the future while strengthening their spirit during prayer. Prayer is a form of meditation, and it's edifying when you do it regularly.

A real woman prays over herself and her family.

QUEEN ESTHER

It's necessary to take time out from the world. It allows us to pray and to seek strength from the Creator. This is commonly referred to as meditation. In the Bible, you'll read of instances when prayer was performed with incense or sacrifices. These types of prayers often took place before wars. Most importantly, there were countless miracles that came after a devoted prayer. Queen Esther prayed and fasted for her people when she knew they were going to be annihilated. She prayed to have an increase in courage and wisdom.

Queen Esther's spiritual prowess saved her people. We're going to need women like her today to save our kings from continuing to throw their lives away. A great woman is a woman of resilience. She won't allow a man who has fallen to remain on the floor. A man needs your gentle touch and voice to give him peace. It allows him to think clearly and conquer his world. Your love may be the only love he knows.

Queen Esther (born Hadassah) had to go into prayer before she could accomplish her opus maximus. It was to protect her culture, family, and an entire community. The queen had to fast for two days and request that all her fellow Jewish people do the same. She knew she had to seek God's wisdom within her prayer to know exactly what to do. The wrong move would've led to the demise of all her people. It wasn't going to be one of those, "as I lay my head down to sleep…" kind of prayers. It had to be one of those prayers that caused everyone in the castle to feel her vibrations.

QUEEN VASHTI

It's hard to increase your faith as a couple when you don't praise each other. Children, as well as grown adults, need to be celebrated because it makes us feel important. The "Words of Affirmation" love language is the most powerful gift that God gave us to share with each other. It's an impartation of love. When you neglect to put your man first, he'll stop placing you first unless he is wet behind the ears.

For example, Queen Vashti, a very beautiful but stubborn woman, caused King Xerxes to get rid of her. The king made room for a woman of which he was destined to meet. This, ultimately, was Queen Esther. The Persian King Xerxes was one of the most powerful kings in ancient times. His empire was so vast that he was known as King of Babylon, being named rather as King of Persia and Media, Great King, King of Kings (Shahanshah), Pharaoh of Egypt, and King of Nations. In the action movie *300*, King Xerxes was the warrior king with the gold chains.

Once she obtained the crown, Queen Vashti thought she was entitled to the throne forever without having to serve her king. This proves that once you have the mate you've been praying for, you should continue serving and uplifting each other. What someone doesn't appreciate about you, there is someone else waiting for the opportunity. *The Great Gatsby* is a perfect example of this except for the fact that his opportunity to reunite with his lost love was only temporary.

Queen Vashti threw her own lavish party for the ladies at the royal palace. Meanwhile, her husband was on the other end of the estate in a festive spirit with his own opulent seven-day party, right after his 180-day party was over. According to records, the royal courtyard was regally decorated with blue and white cotton curtains tied by thick cords of purple linings and silver rings.

Gold and silver couches stood on mosaic pavement made of mother-of-pearl marble. Drinks were served in gold goblets of different styles and filled with the finest wine in Persia, reflecting the king's generosity and military success. This must've been a beautiful sight to see. All the armies of Persia and Media were in attendance, as well as the governors, empresses, and noblemen of the provinces. They were there to partake in the festivities and, of course, to network. Everything was as smooth as cucumbers on ice, up until the seventh day of the after-party.

On the seventh day, King Xerxes wanted his guests to gaze at the beauty of his wife. She was the crème de la crème of her day. Back then, as well as today, a leader being seen with his wife represented stability in the public's eyes. Stability is power. Citizens are more comfortable in a stable kingdom. That's why ninety percent of presidents in any country around the world are married before they begin campaigning. It's great for public relations, pictures, and the press eats it up! The image of a family together is priceless. It paints a positive picture in the minds and hearts of those that lay their eyes on them, especially our youth.

Queen Vashti knew that leaving her party guests to meet her husband's royal guests would've been a sign of submission to her husband's power. He knew that as well, but that good ole friend EGO got the best of the queen. The queen must have been drop-dead gorgeous for the king to go through all that trouble to show off his trophy wife.

I could imagine her saying to the women at her party:

"This fool done lost his rabbit mind. You ladies better drink up and enjoy being pampered while it lasts. My man is going to lose his whole kingdom riches with these over the top parties. I barely made it through the first four months. How many more hangovers can I wake up to?"

A good man will expect you to stand by his side through rain or shine. He should be willing to do the same — and if not, then kick him to the curb immediately. Selfishness is a curable disease that takes great effort to change. The physical support you show expresses an immense amount of love you have for him and his vision. It's one thing to say and text, "I love you" or "I support you," but there is no substitute to showing it. Even when you're not there physically, the spirit of your heart will make your presence felt. Queen Vashti no longer cared for King Xerxes's energy. Her actions clearly spoke, so he had to oust her from the castle and find a new wife.

The king was advised by his royal council to seek a new wife by gathering 1,000 virgin women within his empire to marry. The king pampered all the women and spared no expense. The mademoiselles spent months preparing for the mother of all beauty pageants. This preparation consisted of getting bathed in oil of myrrh for the first six months and then another half a year sitting around sweet odor ointments.

Both the queen's and king's egos were in the way of them building an empire together. It is impossible to elevate to a higher level of consciousness and spirituality when two people are stuck on themselves instead of inspiring each other. In most cases, when you're constantly uplifting your partner's spirit through kind words and favors, the other person is inclined to return the favor. It's guaranteed to create more smiles than frowns.

HIGHER LEVELS

A king operating on a higher level will want a queen who can think with the emotions of her heart and not her ego. A king will know he can trust you with confidential matters because you've proven you can be trusted. He has peace in knowing you'll put his feelings, thoughts, and actions ahead of your own. I pray he has proven himself to you as well.

There are levels in courtship, dating, relationships, and marriage. The longer you're together, the more you can cultivate love for each other, praying power, and trust. This type of couple will make the necessary sacrifices (which include dumping excess baggage off their love flight) so that the relationship can grow stronger. It has the capability of reaching a higher level of God consciousness. This allows both partners to pray in sync and tap into the messages and signals that God (and the universe) channel your way. The two of you will be able to create miracles and little gods. Beautiful children will be born because of the sacrifices made in your relationship.

NOURISH HIS SPIRIT

A man without a wife is just a man with a mind filled with great ideas and wishful thinking. A wife will turn those dreams into reality through prayerful prayers. Women are born to give birth to ideas. You are natural miracle makers. Women naturally want to attach themselves to something or someone who will be great one day. Your role has always been to give life to ideas and dreams that are on the horizon to live a fulfilled life. Something must manifest. This is how it's been since the days of Auset and Ausar in Ancient Africa 33,000 to 50,000 years ago. It's your calling to turn an ordinary man into a great one, but you must choose the king that you want to crown.

The enemy will try to take away your dreams and imagination; that is his job. One of your goals as a woman is to help your man create action steps toward his dream. Push him to carry the fiery torch of your family's legacy in his hands, even if you must hold it up for him. He is the natural leader and defender of the home, so his vision must be as clear as possible for him to lead the family correctly, especially when times get rough. If you are confronted with a battle as a unit, the energy you give him through your prayers, home-cooked meals, good loving, and words will galvanize him to take the proper action.

Place your hands on your king while he sleeps and whisper prayers of blessings upon him. Envision your graceful words going deep into his spirit. See your words enveloping his body like a shield.

"As Above, So Below."

The phrase "As above, so below" represents the belief that order is the first law of Heaven. African high culture civilizations, such as Ancient Kemet and Kush, believed in this concept. The full favor of God doesn't show up for a man until *the good wife* comes into the picture. Because a woman's feminine energy represents heaven anyway, a man is marrying heaven on earth. I believe it's because of the spiritual strength: two gods are stronger than one. Their brain cells, faith, and courage are all multiplied by two. Nature is always correct because only women have the power to give birth.

Metaphysically, it's also accurate because it represents the perfect life balance. It's the key to life. It's created once the unification of the feminine and masculine energy is spawned into action. Two worlds combine to become one. Two little gods uniting to create a desired reality on earth as in the sky – as above, so below. As it is in heaven, let it be on earth. The powers of the heavens are at your disposal. As the "Mother of the Universe," you can bind any evil spirit away from you and your family. There could be spirits running in your dream king's family for generations. If you're not willing to go to war as his Spiritual Queen, then do not open Pandora's Box by sleeping with him, cooking for him, and kissing him. These are three very powerful sacred ceremonial acts that open portals from his life into yours.

A Woman of Her Word

A real man of God will want a faith-filled queen as his wife without a shadow of doubt. He knows that he can go to war with you by his side and be confident that you will catch what he misses and vice versa. He knows he would forfeit his inheritance if he creates a union with a woman who has little to no faith at all. This is a great advantage to all my sisters who understand the value that they have on God's green earth. It is for this reason that rulers of antiquity went out of their way to seek special women who could give birth to their dreams and keep the family's legacy alive. A king will search far and wide for this special woman and be willing to risk all he possesses to create a world with you. All that was sacrificed will come back tenfold.

Furthermore, keeping your word to someone is just as important as the words you're speaking into the world. For a man to trust you, he must know that your spoken word is as good as gold — not your text messages. He doesn't have to doubt that you will do what you say you will do. You will count on each other in many areas of life. Your honesty is the key to unveiling the hidden chambers of his heart. Finding a woman of her word is extremely rare, and these types of women are nearly extinct. Say what you mean, and mean what you say. Trust significantly helps to open the lines of communication.

Let's tighten up!

"Exercise your faith muscles, and put your dukes up!"
- Prophetess Yvette Brinson

STAGES OF LOVE

Once trust is accomplished, then there is room for the 5 A's and righteous love to grow. According to the "Saving Your Marriage Before It Starts" premarital workshop by relationship and marriage counselors Drs. Les and Leslie Parrot, there are five gradual stages of love.

1. The Romance Stage

Steaming romance is at the start of every relationship/marriage. Couples are so into each other during this hot time that they forget their own identity. We are so intoxicated by raging hormones and God's permission to get down with the get down. This phase is the climax most marriages yearn to reach further down the road but seldom do.

2. The Power Struggle Stage

Once the two get off their love high, reality hits. This is a tug-of-war over the dominant role in the relationship. The person they were so deeply in love with doesn't look so perfect and sweet anymore. Couples with huge egos never get past this stage, not alive at least. One perfect example is Frank Sinatra's marriage to the gorgeous Ava Gardner. Sinatra left his previous wife for a woman he had too much in common with, and he realized that the grass wasn't any greener. Ava and Frank were caught up in trying to prove their point at any cost. After five years of a roller coaster ride, they paid the price with their marriage in 1957. Their spirits had a hard time getting along.

You will still have to want that electrical voltage that only your mate brings. Both sides must come to an agreement (not to agree to disagree) and understand their role in the relationship determined by each other. A man knows the woman runs the show, and he is there to support her; however, there will be times when the man must take charge and the woman will submit to his authority. It's the ability to share the power in the relationship that makes it great! When this isn't the case, she will feel repressed and depressed, and then digresses from the relationship.

3. Cooperation Stage

Couples who have reached this level of love are smooth sailing for now. They have a complete understanding that neither one of them are going to change completely. They are willing to compromise for the sake of the relationship. Just because we've been doing certain things for a long time, doesn't necessarily make them right. For instance, running late for every engagement, playing loud obscene music during early morning or late hours, or physically abusing children with belts. Get rid of old family traditions that no longer work and build new healthy traditions with your mate.

Try starting the mornings with prayer, while playing classical or gospel music to start the day. Instead of hitting children, try speaking to them in a calm manner and take away what they adore, such as their favorite foods/snacks and toys.

4. Mutuality Stage

Reaching the mutual love stage for each other gives both people involved the opportunity to reach a new level of ecstasy in lovemaking with your minds. At this level, you realize you are making love just by looking into each other's eyes. Even a simple walk on the beach underneath the sun or moon can be an exhilarating experience for a spiritually connected couple. Love is very much as spiritual as it is physical.

The shift from stage three was difficult enough, but this level is a miracle. Reaching this level of consciousness demonstrates that you are one unit and feel secure about your position in the world together. The woman's emotional roller coaster becomes as relaxing as driving Miss Daisy. The man's temper tantrum evolves into just a pout. Your vibrations are balancing together into a smooth rhythm. Most couples can only dream of reaching this level due to the consistent waste of energy used to bicker and nitpick, and the stress that the world brings.

5. Co-Creativity Stage

Stage five is for the grown folks who are much older, retired, and seek to enjoy the rest of their lives together. This sense of reality allows them to develop a rare kind of energy — co-creativity. There are no doubts, insecurities, and threats to their immediate happiness. This creates an overflow of genuine happiness, kindness, love, and intimacy. Free to do whatever, whenever they please because of the sense of security that you give him. In return, he gives you equality. You realize the rarity of your love and the duty to help others see the light of love in this dark world. Now, it's your responsibility to turn on some lights…possibly for your whole community. Love will spread like wildflowers! You are the stars that will illuminate everywhere that you go.

Love is going to change over time. Love isn't a stone; therefore, it will not remain stagnant. There will be times when your love plane will fly high and times when it will fly low. Turbulence is to be expected from family, careers, and life. It may be easier to love someone during one season and then notice it gets tougher during the next. That's okay if you both are prepared by talking it out ahead of time so that you can work it out. The day you stop communicating is the premier sign that the relationship is headed in the wrong direction. It's wrong to just jump out of a man's life without forewarning. There are women today who have mastered disappearing acts while having a man's heart in their hands. This makes it extremely difficult for anyone to love again, but there are people out there, like myself, who are suckers for love. They will do anything to keep someone who symbolizes love for them.

RIGHTEOUS LOVE

"There is hardly any enterprise which is started with such tremendous hopes and expectations, and yet, which fails so regularly, as love."[1]*-Erich Fromm*

People have the misconception that righteous love happens by coincidence or chance. The art of love must be learned, practiced, and honed like a skill. Point to any lasting relationship or marriage, and they'll tell you that they worked at being a better person for their spouse and for themselves. Combining their energies, passion, and intimacy allows growth for a fulfilling, healthy, and miracle-making relationship. That is what you want, right? Well then, let's get it!

The right woman will lead a man into his destiny. The wrong woman will keep him at the bottom. One of the ways a queen will be able to push a man forward is by having premonitions of things to come. People get so caught up in looking for opportunities to advance their bank accounts and careers, but we would all be able to move way ahead in life if we could avoid the dangers around the corner. Problems usually cause a series of setbacks and are followed by a misdirection of our energy, time, and money. The mistakes are what hold us back in life. A man needs a woman at his side who can help him figure things out and put together a winning formula. You could be what's missing in his equation. Some men need that help more than others, so it's going to require a lot of patience, spiritual strength, and righteous love on your part.

WOMAN OF VIRTUE

A real man knows he will have to sacrifice many things to find a virtuous queen. Any male can find a fine, good-looking woman, or even a prostitute on the street corner. Yet, he doesn't want a woman who is always open like a corner store. A woman worth having will become an inconvenience, because a king knows he will have to go out of his way to get her. He will open the car door for her, pull out her chair before she sits down at home or restaurants, and become her private security guard when out in public.

A woman who possesses dignity, character, cooking skills, and a business mindset is considered one in a million. Together with home values, good health, and education, she isn't going to be easy to find. It's a treasure hunt to find such a virtuous woman. Some men think it's easier to win the lottery. A man may have to travel to another city to find you, or even another country. The worst case scenario is that he may have to time travel to another lifetime to find you — like in the classic love story *Forever Young*. He knows there is no way that he'll ever reach his destiny without your spirit. One can have all the wealth in the world, but there will be a void in every real man until he is married and/or has children. Your heart is the key to unlock the next dimension of blessings. He'll wait and search for you because you are worth it. However, your value can only be determined by you.

POWER OF ONE

By now you should know if you have the heart of a lioness. If you do, then he'll be able to see his reflection in you. This is assuming that he is a strong man of honor. A faith-filled queen is one with herself, Mother Nature, and God's grace flowing inside every atom in her body. Grace gives you the ability to do what you have no power, scholarship, or experience to do. In many parts of the world, especially Africa, they believe that God and nature are one and the same. God is everywhere.

"The wind, the water, the fire, and the earth. She was Mother Earth, Mother of Everything and she had the power to, through her essence, move freely throughout the universe; frequently flying from heaven to earth."[2]

They believed that men could only reach the pinnacle of being through the spirit of his woman. Proverbs 18:22 states: "A man who finds a good wife has found treasure and favor from the Lord." My interpretation of this scripture is: "A man who finds a wife has found heaven on earth."

Furthermore, if my research on antiquity is correct, a man that finds a good wife has found a connection to heaven.

SACRED TEMPLE OF HEAVEN

Ancient civilizations believed that feminine fluids were essential elements of life-giving nourishment. Your body was considered the "Sacred Temple of Heaven," a blessed rainmaker, and the home of the life-creating force. The Ankh symbol (which is the original cross) has an "O" on top of the cross, representing the woman's womb.

The bottom half of the Ankh is the man's phallus, representing the masculine energy. With the woman on top (heaven) and the man holding up the woman on the bottom (earth), it creates the perfect balance. It represents the key to life. It's like water raining down from heaven replenishing the earth. Notice that it's the woman (feminine principle) on top and not the bottom, because in order for a woman to manifest her fullest potential as a queen she must be free and comfortable. Only a real man, who isn't controlled by his ego, would be comfortable with allowing his woman to be in charge. Men must accept their gentle side or they will live an unbalanced life, as we consist of the female and male principle.

SPIRITUAL TUNE-UP

Relationships must be tuned up like a piano. Pianos should be adjusted up to twice a year to achieve a concert pitch. Relationships require tune-ups frequently to obtain that high frequency level of understanding, compassion, communication, and love. The day you take your companion for granted, you will leave your relationship open to chaos: low levels of understanding, communication, and love. Communication is vital in relationships, wars, and business. We all know that constant silence is the first sign that things are heading downhill. All it takes is some time, energy, and intentional focus to get the rhythm of your hearts back on track.

CHESS NOT CHECKERS

Relationships are like chess, which is a game of strategy. For those of you who enjoy or understand the basics of chess, you comprehend that, while the king is the most important, the queen is the most powerful piece on the board. Everything evolves around the royal couple. The rooks, knights, bishops, and pawns all beckon to her call — including the king. They all have a different value, and the queen is the most powerful with nine points. In reality, the queen is worth the most points on the chessboard. The game isn't over until the king, worth zero points, has been captured. It's critical to know how to protect him with the queen. The creators of chess, the Kemetians, must have venerated women — the female principle. The king isn't worth a single point. It's not a coincidence that the Kemetians created the most popular board game in the world.

Are you interested in being a pawn or the queen? You must be conscious of the energies of those around you. Ask yourself: what type of spirit are they operating in? Better yet, what kind of portal will they open once you exchange time and energy with them: good or evil? Understand the value of what and whom God has blessed you. Having awareness of surrounding spirits puts us in a position to ascertain what we desire. Separating yourself from the negative energy that drains your spirit allows you to seek out the good folks who will edify you.

MAKING ROOM FOR YOUR DREAMS

An anointed woman of God isn't dreaming about a man. An anointed woman of God dreams for her man." ~ Pastor Jamal H. Bryant.

A woman is going to dream for her man and with her man, despite the circumstances. She's going to speak blessings into his world with prayers. She's going to give him words of encouragement with her benevolence. She's going to send blessings his way around the clock, even as he sleeps.

Cute little girls with fancy dreams become women with vision. This vision gives women the gift of clairvoyance. This gift must be protected by the strength and presence of a father, brother, uncle, or husband — her king. This is often hindered due to baggage of depression and years of emotional imbalances due to the lack of a spiritually strong, caring masculine figure in their life.

The baggage could derive from past pains due to relationships, ex-boyfriends who are still in the picture years after you've split up, or serious broken family issues. It's not only a turn off, but it's also a crying shame. A man cannot — and will not — take you seriously knowing that your heart is still with your ex-boyfriend, ex-husband, or your family who has more control over your relationship than the two of you do. You have the whole future ahead of you, but you're still holding on to the past that can't do a thing for you except hold you back in a time capsule of hurt. This is not the equation that will add up to a happy life with the man of your dreams. At some point, you will have to drop those unwanted bags of hurt that are holding up your flight from taking off!

SPIRITUAL LOVE FLIGHT

During a love flight, women represent the private jet while a family is represented by a jetliner (mother and children with no father figure present). Of course, women can be the pilots and are, in fact, flying commercial flights now. However, not even a strong woman should be flying the plane and monitoring the passengers herself. The roles must be split. It takes two.

Now let's say that a man is the pilot, the captain of your flight. The female principle is still represented by the vessel, which is the private jet. The jet can look like a million dollars — sleek with gold pinstripes, an elevator, and leather seats. The captain can have all the accolades of a great pilot. If the pilot (masculine energy) and the plane (feminine energy) can't combine their energies together as one force, then neither of them will elevate from the ground. They will both remain in the hangar looking crazy. A man should empower his woman with his energy and fill her up with jet fuel. The jet cannot fuel itself, just like a woman can't fill herself up with her love's masculine energy. The woman must have the right energy from a man to fuel her with positivity, uplift her spirit with courage, and give her an electrical charge when it is needed to take flight. The man cannot fulfill his destiny without a vessel, which is you, his queen. He is going to need your divine spirit so you can reach your destiny together. You absolutely both need each other.

The combustion created because of you both being on the same wavelength will cause your flight to not only be smoother, but to also go further and faster. You must trust in each other and read the signs before you board the journey you're preparing to embark on in life. Being able to elevate beyond the physical realm will help you and your king overcome many issues that the world will present since the two of you are high in the sky. Instead of looking up at your problems, you'll look down on them from on top of the world. Your problems are beneath you, not above you.

THE IDEAL HELPMATE

The helpmate subject is interesting because it often develops into a helping issue. Many failed relationships, including marriages, never get beyond the helping phase. Women are natural nurturers. Caring for others and anything with life is in your DNA. In many situations, women naturally empathize with other people's feelings.

It makes perfect sense women were the first healers, agriculture scientists, and zoologists of the world. You can nurture a plant, tree, wounded animal, baby, and man. It becomes difficult to be in a relationship when you can't be your natural self. Our genes have been altered in our society for the past seventy to eighty years. Women's nurturing nature has become domineering.

Nowadays, some women don't just nurture. They want complete control. I often hear (and see) more women who want to wear both the pants and skirts in the relationships, business world, and in the homes. Women have become controlling and get an attitude when their man doesn't comply with their excessive demands. A sensible man doesn't want any attitude, so he does what you say to avoid the tension. I'm a true supporter of women's empowerment, success, and all that good stuff, but what about the spirit of our men? A lot of men feel unimportant and less of a man when their queen makes more money. This gives her all the power in the relationship, as money is perceived as power. Spirits gets broken in these incidences.

Couples who don't have a higher dimension of purpose fizzle out by getting bored with each another because they don't need the help anymore. That passionate fire will get blown away when the windy storms of life come along. Whatever brought you two together at this point will not last. In fact, you may even question your relationship.

Keeping the Fire Lit

After years of marriage, you don't need each other's assistance as much, if at all. You both will be able to iron your own clothes, make your own meals, and make your own breakfast in bed, which defeats the purpose of the whole idea. The more time you spend away from your spouse, the greater the border between you will grow until your two worlds are completely divided. A house divided cannot stand. Imagine a castle without pillars or an eagle without wings. This is the status a marriage evolves to when you aren't holding each other up. Someone who yearns for your king's energy will replace the energy you're lacking from each other.

Women will adapt to any vision of the man. If he has no vision, he will lead you and the kids straight to destruction. If your twin flame is a visionary, what idea does he have that you can protect? Is it children, a business idea, an invention, a home, investments, and so forth? If there isn't anything, then he isn't the right person. He is the frog you should not crown.

Now, of course, all men aren't visionaries. You're going to need a vision to latch onto to cultivate the keeping power to remain together for the long term and for eternity. To keep the fiery passion lit, your relationship will have to become more spiritual than physical.

Pray and spend time with God. Both the feminine and masculine principles of the Creator will begin to plant seeds into your womb. Your focus is to fertilize those seeds of your king with your sacred fluids, creative energy, wisdom, and powerful words of affirmation.

Dear Queen,

*Every spiritual man would want to have
a woman that will pray for him and
with him. It makes the relationship a
little more enticing and interesting.*

CHAPTER 5

A KING BUILDER

"Are you his backbone or backbreaker?"

Your encouragement is never-ending and creates eternal happiness. As tough as a man may think he is, men need morale boosting throughout our lives; an occasional pep talk to keep our vision intact works wonders. At some point of your life, the art of cheerleading will come in handy as a friend. A woman's energy is the difference between a man defeating his Goliath or succumbing to him.

In the Bible, King David's motivation for fighting Goliath was King Saul's daughter, Princess Michal. He was going to fight Goliath anyway; however, through gaining the princess's hand in marriage he knew, for a fact, that he would soon become what almost every man desires to be — a bona fide king. It would be a huge blessing to his bloodline for generations to come.

MATRIARCHS

Most men who grew up like myself were raised in the ghetto by a beautiful single mother. This is known as the matriarchal system. These strong women willed their sons to be "the man of the house," which is a man before his time. This is a two-fold problem. First of all, there weren't any real men to teach them how to be a "man," a provider of legal means, or a defender and protector. Second, women are being raised too strong and independent for their own good. Our generation is becoming so bent on trying to prove that women can do what men can do, and it's causing women to lose their gentle uniqueness. Women weren't created to do everything a man can do. Women were created to do everything a man can't do!

Now — when a woman becomes partners with a real man in a home, she may be hesitant to allow him to be a man who will provide and protect her. They will experience a constant friction over power. There's an insurmountable amount of battles to fight out in the world. The last place anyone would want to fight is where their heart is home sweet home. However, it is not her fault, as she never had an example of a collective partnership, or "oppositional unity." This is how Dr. Marimba Ani, African Studies Scholar and anthropologist, defines it. Oppositional unity means women and men aren't here to fight against each other for power or position. We're here to be our best and to help each other reach our destinies.

Many guys are scared away from women who are overtly independent. Furthermore, many males became men by receiving affirmations from our mothers (or female guardians), but not our fathers. The problem with this scenario is that many of us, unless we are raised up in a good church, aren't taught how to focus our energy in a positive manner. We are not educated on how we must tame our emotions when life's circumstances get a little crazy. Little boys were taught that when we stick it in a girl, a baby comes out nine months later. And when it comes to fighting, boys are taught not to lose. We are taught to beat the living crap out of anyone who talked about our mothers or tried to take anything away from us. Making decisions based on our emotions without thinking logically leads to dangerous results; unfortunately, that's how many of us learn our lesson. A real man and king looks out for his people and community by showing and giving love, but not everyone is taught this principle.

The mother can only do so much when it comes to guiding and encouraging a boy to become a king. He grew up enjoying her breast as an infant and feasting on great dinners as a child. As a man, however, it's time for him to suckle on the breast of his queen (his wife). It's natural for a man to be connected to your breast for sexual enjoyment but, more importantly, to maintain closeness between both is involved. Become his guiding light with your felicitous words of encouragement to avoid the inevitable traps of this cold world. Many of our good, strong, and capable men fall into these traps when they become discouraged.

A woman's confidence in herself can share enough of her love energy to uplift her king. I truly believe that a queen's love energy can reduce the amount of men choosing a life of crime, because a king who knows better will raise young boys to become great men as well. The revolving door of recidivism will be shut for one person at a time.

GIVERS OF LIFE

Hardships often prepare ordinary people for an extraordinary fortune. Men have faced extremely difficult circumstances; therefore, a man will need your tender loving care to heal him back into his natural loving, protective self. Juvenile detention centers and prisons are filled with men who have never experienced a loving woman's gentle touch on their hearts. Sadly, some haven't even experienced this love from their mothers, and they probably never will. Queens, you not only possess the DNA of our ancestors in your wombs, but you also carry the ability to raise kings from the dead. Resurrect their dead spirits from dormancy! Your value as a queen gives you the power to change a man's fortune. Think of yourself as the givers of life.

Fortune comes from a Latin deity, Fortuna, the name of a goddess personifying luck or chance.

In the United States, there are more than 2.2 million men in prison. Forty to fifty percent of them are Black men, according to *Huffington Post.*[1] There is a large Hispanic, Caucasian, and Asian population in prison, but the fact remains that Black men lead the pack. The leaders of our communities — our kings — are not only incarcerated but also exiled from their families, neighborhoods, and society. This results in potential kings and adolescent males becoming incarcerated, exiled, and pushed out of society, thus never reaching their kingdom ship. Don't get it twisted — some of these males deserve to be locked up or even put under the jails, but that is only a small percentage of them.

Our young women and men need to be hidden from the harshness of the real world until they are ready to go out on their own. Eagles don't even leave the nest right after they hatch. Our youth are being thrown out prematurely to shake hands with the sharks and wolves of the world. This will not happen if the parents are selfless enough to put their energies together to protect, teach, and nurture their young until they are ready.

I blame this epidemic on the system that created this problematic political-socio environment. There must be something fictitious about our culture, upbringing, and values. Since 1985, the number one growing population in prison is female, both young and old. As a matter of fact, there are more than one million women incarcerated, and the number is growing at a high rate.[2] It's going to require queens and kings who are conscious of the current epidemic to uplift our young daughters out of this hellhole they are in now.

Somewhere along the line, we gave up on them and they ultimately gave up on themselves. They gave up on their dreams and went for the free-for-all life of crime, which wasn't free at all. The juvenile detention centers can attest to that. Someone wasn't there to catch them falling out of the nest at the beginning of their life's journey. When life gets tough for a man, one of the best solutions is the gentleness of a female, such as kind words from his young daughter, the love energy from his queen, a home-cooked meal made with love, or the wisdom of his grandmother to revive his spirit and soul. The combination of all four feminine energy sources will create a vibrational frequency to combat any challenge in life.

HARDSHIP BUILDS CHARACTER

When the ocean is rough, fear is the rock on which we split. Hate is the shore on which many of us are stranded. When we become fearful, our judgment is as unreliable as a ship without a compass. When we hate, we have unshipped the rudder. If we ever stop to meditate on what the gossipers are saying, we have allowed the haters to make us miss enjoying the relaxation of the beach.

A man of vision will need help remaining focused in a world filled with distractions and adversity. Keep his mind on the great and splendid goals the both of you desire to accomplish. Then, he will eventually find your reflection in his mirror. He'll unconsciously seize the opportunities required for the fulfillment of your desire. Picture the able, earnest, useful person you desire your king to be and your thoughts and love will transform him into the individual you so admire. The same concept works for any given goal. Thought is supreme, so don't just think. It's often better to just do it.

Your character is the result of two things: mental attitude and the way we spend our time when no one is looking. What we think and what we do makes us who we are. As a female develops into womanhood, it's critical that she completes tasks all the way to the end and keeps her word without giving up. She will develop rare virtues and become sought after by men of quality, especially in today's society.

> *"Whenever you go out of doors, draw your chin in, carry your crown with your head high, and fill the lungs to the utmost; drink in the sunshine; greet your friends with a smile, and put soul into every hand-clasp." - Essayist and publisher Elbert Hubbard*

BUILDING YOUR HOME & KEEPING IT

Men don't want to come to a house. We want to come *home*. A king needs his woman to "quiet his mind." This means you will use precaution with the words you choose. After a long day of work, no one wants to come home to a chatterbox of complaints. A woman who nags too much about herself, her friend's problems, or issues she may have with her man will be a hindrance to his peace of mind. Yes, men are prepared to listen to you. Be mindful not to stab him with your words, however, and your callous actions when you're angry.

Regardless of how many kids, history, and plans the two of you have together — it can all go up in smoke. Men are scared away due to negative energy cooking in the home. You will increase the chances of him walking out of the door to seek the temptations calling his name every day; he won't return. Hopefully, he doesn't become king in another home while he's M.I.A. (Missing In Action). If you're not careful, you'll end up completely ignoring the critical issues that your king is facing. These issues are possibly driving him nuts. Some guys can be complete jerks when they're having their mood swings. Get a sense of his vibrations and just be as submissive as possible when you sense he isn't "himself." Try being extra kind and understanding of his problems, while talking to him about the things you know he enjoys and loves. This always helps me open up when I'm not in a talkative mood. These things are geared toward building him up and, most importantly, it shows your endearing support.

Males and females are genetically different. The male and female energies are extremely powerful if used appropriately. The power of our words cannot be underestimated, and women should use the divine power of their words to increase the positive energy of their home; in other words, not to decrease it. Use your words to direct the blessings you want to see over your man, not to break him down. After all, he's the one in charge of protecting you from harm, which is kind of important.

SET THE ATMOSPHERE

If you're married or in a serious relationship with a man who has low vibrations, then you are obligated to give him some inspiration. Be cautious about how you set the tone for the day in the morning hours. Speak only good things — no complaints or arguments. The energy in the morning is so powerful that it carries throughout the day into the evening. Even if there isn't really anything good that comes to mind, speak something positive anyway. For instance, you can say: "It's going to be a great day!" And it will come true because you spoke it into existence. You must believe it. Your positive energy will transcend into his mind, affecting his attitude toward you, himself, and the world. As the woman of the house, the rhythm of the home is up to you. Are we going to have a good day or a bad one? You are the thermostat. When the day starts with an argument, you'll notice that a heat wave of strife will blow your natural high all day.

Now let's say you've turned things around by consciously thinking nothing but good thoughts toward your king. The frequency of your day will fizzle out all negativity coming from neighbors, coworkers, and the day-to-day grind. You'll notice that the vibe throughout the day will be so high that nothing in the world can drag you down. Your love plane together will continue to fly higher and higher on course to your destination.

POWER SHIFT

We have a population filled with women who are beautiful and successful. They are often overly aggressive with their men, children, family, and themselves. The paradigm has shifted. At this moment in time, women are the primary hunters in some homes, which changes the dynamic of power quite a bit. Could you imagine lionesses chilling under the shade while the lions go out to hunt? It would be an interesting sight to see. Millennial women weren't taught to balance their aggressiveness with logic and love, which takes patience in a society that barely has time to do anything that isn't in a smartphone app. That aggression leads men to feel they are more tolerated than loved or wanted, causing clashes between the two worlds instead of a smooth merge. By the same token, Millennial men are learning to allow the women to have more power and control in the relationship.

Nevertheless, I love a woman who allows a man to be a man in the relationship. She won't make it her prerogative to overpower his authority in every single situation. It's no different from a man who intentionally wants to suppress his woman's freedom. This kind of relationship turns into a prison where righteous love will suffocate until there is no light to shine between the two of you. Imagine standing in a dark room with a tiny glimmering light bulb in your hands that is blocked from letting its light glow. Once the relationship gets so depressing, and seems as if it's beyond repair, you'll notice that there isn't even a spark of light left.

When life hits a man with an immensely hard blow, like taking out his finances and any means of reaching his dream, we tend to give up on ourselves and stop believing. Your presence will be most appreciated and needed in the trenches of life — with you in his face, spirit, and on his mind willing him to hang in there. Men can't do it without women. During the days of Kemet, for a man to become king, the queen had to crown him king first (unless the previous kingdom is overthrown). Usually the incumbent king is bigger, richer, and well protected, which pretty much means the challenger has the odds stacked against him. Your words of encouragement and the vision shared upon him will give that extra edge to defeat the odds and become king.

BUILDING A CHAMPION

Have you ever watched any movies from the classic *Rocky®* franchise? This great boxing movie — produced for approximately one million dollars — grossed more than 225 million dollars at the box office back in 1976 and racked up more than one billion during the six-film franchise. In part two, Rocky Balboa — played by Sylvester Stallone — had a rematch with Mr. T (Laurence Tureaud). Rocky got his butt whooped badly and, to make matters worse, his coach Mickey passed away before the fight. This was due to a heart attack in the locker room. It was a sad moment indeed, but a special moment in the classic film also happened because of the two knock-out punches to his spirit.

Rocky's wife (played by the beautiful Talia Share) watched her man get his rear end handed to him and witnessed her husband's spirit toiling in pain from losing his only mentor, trainer, and championship title. He had plans to retire, but he wanted a rematch with Mr. T in honor of Mickey's death. No matter what he did, he just couldn't get back into his zone or rhythm. This is crucial for teachers, athletes, attorneys, pastors, writers, and so forth. The zone occurs when your thoughts and energy align to produce the physical reality you wish to manifest before and during a given task. This state of mind allows focused athletes to get a tunnel vision — one that is laser focused.

Moreover, the flashy boxer Apollo Creed tried to shake off Rocky's depressed spirit by training him. His friend tried to give him words of encouragement and even flew him from Philly to California to support him. One day, Mrs. Balboa was present at one of Rocky's sad practices on the beach. She decided to step in to give him a reality check. She was all up in his face and challenged him to snap out of his depression. It was a very intense moment in the movie, and that scene continues to inspire me every time I watch the film today.

Even though this was only an old 1970s Hollywood film, it epitomizes what's going on today. Many men are giving up on their dreams and passions after taking a hit. Some men are fortunate to have the energy of their queen to encourage them to stay positive and strong. It's only natural for a queen to want her king to WIN!

MAGIC OF UNITY

I have a theory called two sides of affection: positive and negative. Some people habitually attract an unbelievable amount of stress, problems, and drama. They've never had a quality relationship that lasted several years due to their aggressive nature and negativity. Relationships that don't have a higher purpose other than self-gratification for being together will not last — sex isn't enough. You must have the consciousness that your purpose together is to do great things in life, not to just work, have sex, and eat well together.

You should get together as a union because something greater than you will be birthed. When you both are conscious that you are together to conceive something greater than yourselves, something of a greater or higher value will manifest. Couples who don't have a higher dimension of purpose fizzle out and get bored with each other because they stop helping and uplifting each other. They lack staying power. When couples stop wasting their time and energy arguing, they can place energy into their great ideas. That's the magic of unity.

Energy will attract its own kind of energy, whether positive or negative. The universe reciprocates the energy we put out into the world. Take the time to observe people's energy, and you'll be able to draw these people out. Negative people should be avoided or fed with a long spoon. They have toxic energy, and all you can really do is pray for them. Point them in the right direction. Like the wise words of the late great singer Nina Simone, "*You've got to learn to leave the table when love's no longer being served.*" You can show a horse the water but can't make 'em drink it. A man with this type of negative energy should be avoided by any means necessary. Your space and energy is sacred, and it should be treated as such. Your time, space, and energy shouldn't be open to everyone like a corner store.

On the flip side of this equation are women who have an abundance of high energy, favor, and grace. Great things always seem to follow them. Career opportunities, lasting relationships, money falling out of the sky, and happiness are associated with them. They even speak positively when they are having a bad day. I have been blessed to be in a relationship with a couple of women who possess this kind of aura. They are often taken advantage of because they usually don't realize how much of a blessing they are in a relationship. Men fortunate enough to keep this type of woman in their lives are blessed. Queens like this aren't easy to come by, but they do exist.

Your divine powers as a woman are so strong that you can solely lift a man up or bring his whole empire down. When a woman chooses to help a man with his business or project, you'll see that she'll work diligently as if she had come up with the idea herself. Women will give their energy wherever their graceful presence is appreciated and make it work. Your heart, mind, and spirit are wide open to serve the man you choose to crown as your king. I just wish more women were wiser about who they crown as their king. That's

why it's important for women to understand the divine powers God
has bestowed upon them.

THE CROWNING

The crown was worn to distinguish royalty from the common
folks in large crowds. Over time, gems were placed on the queen's
and king's headpieces. The issue is that our queens are with unproven
males pretending to be kings. In many cases, women are mainly
crowning clowns, frogs and hyenas — imposters turning their dreams
into nightmares. Their palace, over time, transitions into a dungeon
while their true king is traveling the Seven Seas in search for them. A
true king will become the leader who will help guide and focus your
energy. Together, both of your dreams will manifest. You'll know he is
a true king when you've seen him conquer his challenges with poise;
feelings of safety and appreciation are both associated with him.

For a real man to experience fulfillment, he must accomplish
the goals he set out to attain; his manhood is tied into the ability to
produce and provide for himself. With the love from a good woman,
we are energized with a higher purpose. This is to serve you, love as
much as possible, and protect you with every bit of strength we can
muster. Naturally, in our youth, men are satisfied by serving themselves. As we mature, to become brave battle-tested men, self-gratification no longer satisfies our appetite. We begin to live our life
motivated by the most powerful energy known to humankind —
LOVE. Men want to receive love just as much as women do, but
our greatest need is to give love. Men are at their best when they
are giving. Women are at their best when they are receiving. It's the
perfect balance.

Men are givers of energy, and we hope that the magnetism the woman of our dreams possesses pulls toward us. Most men aren't in fulfilling relationships or don't know how to be committed to a woman. Many never had a father figure take the time to teach them how to live with or treat a woman. And we have women who weren't taught how to live with a man. It's a big headache. We are no good without the loving nature of a woman. When you love a man by showing him that he's appreciated, a sensible man will love you without any resentment. It encourages him to keep giving while he uplifts you instead of taking anything and everything he can from you.

CROWNING YOUR KING

When a woman puts her mouth on a man's penis, she is crowning him. The shaft of the penis is the head and her mouth is the crown piece. The same thing is true with the vagina — the gateway. When she sits on a man's erected penis, her vagina is representing the crown. This sacred act of sex has now bonded the two spirits. If he has evil spirits within him, those spirits will transfer and multiply with your spirits (people you've both been intimate with), whether good or bad. Now, you're officially in his world and he is in yours. There are many one-night stands that take place, and people have no idea what kind of spirits are being injected into their lives. Mess around with the wrong person, and you'll need an exorcism to get rid of those spirits, toxic ideas, and whatever else he left in you and countless other women. This is where sexually transmitted demons come into play.

A woman can crown a man in the four following ways:

1) Her heart

2) Her lips

3) Her vagina

4) Her spirit

The sad part is that most queens have sex without the intention of crowning her mate, her king. It's just casual sex. Women have the power to see the soul of their man while giving him head. Here, you can read his true intentions, the true desires of his heart. The throat area absorbs the unseen energy of a person, place, or thing. It's a great receptor for all energy. When a man is performing oral sex on a woman, he is receiving her pure and uncut energy source. This is coming straight from her power source, which is the womb. It is the gateway to another world: heaven. When she has an orgasm, he is swelling the vortex that moves energy from the spiritual world to the physical world. This energy, used consciously, can heal parts of the body and create miracles. *The Secret Science of the Black Male & Female Sex* book by my friend, T.C. Carrier is a great read to learn more about the sexual energy.

Words come from the throat area and into your environment. Here we are just thinking it's only oral sex. All I am saying is this: if you're going to partake in it, make it worthwhile. Do it for a man who treasures and honors you enough to cherish and marry you. A man who is serious about you will get his ducks in a row to invest his future in you. Money comes and goes, but a good man who focuses on building a life journey with you shows he is worthwhile.

SIDE BY SIDE

The woman is a king builder, but she cannot build up a man to be a king if she is consistently being torn down. When a man finds his queen, he is willing to give you his empire wholeheartedly. All of his dreams, secret ideas, and aspirations will become a reality, thanks to you.

Thomas Sankora, feminist and former President of the West African country Burkina Faso, stated the following in his book *Women's Liberation and the African Freedom Struggle*:

"There can be no proud man without a woman at his side. Every proud man — every strong man — draws his energy from a woman. The endless source of virility is femininity. The endless source, and the key to victories, always lies in the hands of a woman. It is at the side of a woman, sister, or companion that each one of us finds a burst of honor and dignity.[3]

When a man is in love with you: he would bring you the sun, moon, and stars. That's how important a great woman is to a real man. King Nebuchadnezzar of Babylon (reigned 605 BC-562 BC) gave his queen the world. He married Princess Amytis, daughter of King Xerxes I and Queen Amestris of Midian. The new queen was homesick and depressed. History tells us that the king decided to take it upon himself to provide her with a home away from home. To relieve her depression, he recreated her homeland by building an artificial mountain with a rooftop garden at their castle. His love for her opened this massive amount of creative energy. Their marriage was arranged to bring Medes and Babylonia into a peace treaty. There was a purpose greater than the two of them.

A king will do whatever it takes to keep his queen happy. Princess Amytis came from Medes — a land flourishing with mountains, trees, and exotic birds. She ended up in Babylon (center of Iraq) with the sunbaked terrain of Mesopotamia (this is equivalent to a girl from South Florida moving to South Dakota without anything or anyone familiar). King Nebuchadnezzar knew his queen missed her home in Medes. Sensing her depression, he decided to bring Medes to Babylon. He built a royal garden, consisting of an artificial mountain with rooftop gardens, hence, "The Hanging Gardens."[4] Because of the king's desire to please his woman, he built something that ended up becoming one of the Seven Wonders of the World.

The plants were suspended over the heads of spectators and draped over the terraced walls. They cleverly built arches underneath the terraces. The eclectic colored flowers and trees dangling from the walls created an exotic environment. The garden stood at an amazing 400 x 400 feet, as tall as the city walls.

If that wasn't enough, he had to figure out how he was going to water those lustrous trees and plants. This royal garden was a technological challenge, as well as an architectural conquest. They created an irrigation system possibly beyond anything ever created at the time. All this creative energy manifested to please one special woman. Aren't you that special too? Heck yeah, you are!

BUILDING AN EMPIRE

A man will not share his empire with a woman if she has an unstable mind, which will be revealed in her actions. Marrying a double-minded or fickle woman is like putting diamonds and pearls on a pig's snout; it makes no sense whatsoever. If he is wise, then he knows he risks placing his legacy into the hands of a woman who can make it all crumble to rubble like in the City of Pompeii. She can change her mind and disappear one day like a runaway bride. Or worse, she can file for divorce after a few months with the intention of taking everything he's acquired. In many states, a woman is legally entitled to half of her man's estate. You best believe that every man who has his ducks in a row will question whether you will multiply and add to his vision or subtract from it.

You might be the one in the relationship with the empire, such as the living legend, eight-time Grammy award winner Anita Baker. Ms. Baker fought her whole life and moved from foster home to foster home. Eventually, at the age of sixteen, Anita was discovered singing at a nightclub during the 1970s. She had to grind her way to the top of the charts, and she accumulated five platinum albums, along with one gold album under her belt. She was frequently sought after by men for her voice, gorgeous looks, and fortune. After a long divorce, her ex-husband still tried to suck money out of her, as if he was in the struggle with her.

Ladies, examine your man's intentions for wanting to be with you. Is it for your good cooking? Is it the money or how you keep your body fit? If his love for you is based on anything materialistic, then it's time for you to create an exit plan from that relationship. Your energy and time should be geared toward allowing a good man to court you. He may not have the six-figure income, flashy cars, and wardrobe you admire in a man — but those blue-collared men are overlooked the most. If you're going to give a man the best you've got, then you should do your due diligence to discern that he's worth all your treasure.

Let's say that the gentleman courting you is well-established in the business community. Your duty is to fan his business with your spiritual wings of grace. Fan the fires of his imagination with your divine words. The feminine wisdom principle was the impetus for man's quests. A man's business will go from good to great with the support of your feminine touch. An abundance of favor comes to a man when he finds a "good wife."

With the number of entrepreneurs and corporations sprouting up these days, men hope for a woman who can help with their ideas to some degree. There are thousands of companies that shut down every day because of the lack of internal support. Men do not mind having a wife at home tending to the kids while he brings home the bacon, but having a woman who can help him with some of the tasks of operating a business day-to-day is a huge plus. He will save money and get to spend more time with you and vice versa.

However, women these days have more graduate degrees and make more money than the average man. The only problem I see with this scenario is that many women seem to flaunt their money, success, and cars intentionally in the faces of those less fortunate. This especially happens in front of men down on their luck. This display of success is inappropriate and should be frowned upon. A king builder inspires others to be greater.

A woman who can improve the way her man does business, improve the way he carries himself, and help him bring in more money to their empire is a woman well worth fighting for. It's a blessing to run into a woman who increases a gentleman's position with her grace and knowledge. A woman can only exude this glow if she knows her self-worth, not in terms of money but in applicable knowledge.

One night, Beyoncé's "Upgrade You" song was playing on the car radio as I drove my date home from a high school football game. The lyrics made me realize I wanted a queen who complements my style, my vision, my world, and my kingdom. A queen whose presence alone in public will make others want to bless me. She knows it! I know it! The world knows it! Ladies, you need to know that your presence is a blessing too, and embrace it.

BUILDING YOUR WORLD WITH WORDS

A man feels like he's less of a man when he is not able to produce. He feels unwanted, inadequate, and seeks negative ways to manifest his dreams. Instead of focusing on what is positive in his life, such as his family and community, he may seek to destroy the very things he is built to protect, provide, and love. In between the space of positive and negative energy is where you, his queen, come in to point our men in the right direction. Your words are like polished diamonds shining brightly through the dark cave of his soul. Just like decorations drastically improve a home, your positive words and affirmations are the décor that liven up and adorn his spirit.

A woman with a "Jezebel Spirit" will not see the importance of uplifting a man's spirit with her words when he's down, but will seek every opportunity to crush his spirit even more. This way of thinking gives any woman the power to manipulate her man's mind and alter his decision-making. The choice of how you're going to use your divine energy and words is up to you.

In the Bible, soon-to-be king David was going to battle a man who insulted him and his soldiers while they were in a desperate situation looking for food and water. The woman of the house, Abigail, stepped in to mitigate the boiling situation by preventing David from killing her foolish husband, Nabal. Moments after meeting Abigail, David told her, "Blessed be the LORD God of Israel, who sent you this day to meet me; and blessed be your discernment, and blessed be you, who have kept me this day from bloodshed and from avenging myself by my own hand." (1 Samuel 25:33).

The story continues with Abigail blessing David and his soldiers by loading an array of gifts onto their donkeys: two hundred loaves of bread, two jugs of wine, five sheep already prepared, five measures of roasted grain, a hundred clusters of raisins, and two hundred cakes of figs. God used her wisdom to prevent the tragedy of a life being taken away by the rage of men. After seeing her wisdom, David wanted to make her his wife. Her words were powerful enough to stop the person who wanted to stop her husband's heart from beating. If she has the power to stop his heart, then she has the power to increase his heart rate with her words. Our words can be a sword or food for the soul.

The saying, "sticks and stones may break my bones but words will never hurt me" is a lie. Words can and have killed ideas, self-esteem, and the spirit of people since the beginning of time. Words can empower people. Words can create our world as well as destroy it. Words can build a person's self-esteem up so high that they'll begin to have confidence in themselves. A charismatic person depends on the power of his or her words for one simple reason: words are the quickest way to create an emotional reaction.

Words are so elusive that they have the capability of inspiring, elevating, and stirring anger. I was once in a very promising relationship, and you couldn't catch us at a major event without each other. We just had so much in common. She was supportive, caring, and outgoing. She just always knew what to say to brighten up my day from sun-up to sun-down. I consciously even called her my sunshine on numerous occasions. A couple of years into that great relationship, she began to allow the words of a male in her family she highly revered to seep into her spirit, therefore altering her reality. She suddenly began talking differently toward me in a negative sense. The one person's support I'd depended on for a couple of years disintegrated.

I didn't understand until I began paying close attention and reflecting on the words in our conversations. We got along so well in the past, but without warning she wanted to jump ship (more like jump out of our love flight). This new reality was to exclude me from her world without merit. She slowly erased me out of her life. I immediately learned a valuable lesson: pay attention to the people my woman spends her energy and time talking to day to day. Their words will become her words, which will ultimately change my world. A woman's intuition already knows when another woman is doing something unacceptable around her man, and it's her natural instinct to keep her man at a safe distance from another woman. A man must do the same to protect his investment, which is you.

A man can trap you in his fantasy world, promising to purchase you an SL 550 Mercedes Benz, a yacht, and the moon, but he doesn't have to give it to you if you're caught up in his spell of words. A king will back up his words with actions because he knows he must win your confidence, trust, and divine energy to push him into his destiny. A good leader understands the value of your wisdom. He will go out of his way to keep you in his midst. His space. His presence. A man will want you in his life because he knows that you will consistently speak wisdom, love, and prosperity into his life, even when he's acting like a pain in your neck.

Add value to his life by being his best friend and a loyal confidant. Help manifest his goals in life, support his dreams, and lend him moral and mental support in times of trouble.

Your thoughts are expressed through your words, and your words create your reality. My pastor and mother, Prophetess Yvette Brinson, is a powerful weapon in the Kingdom of God. I recall sitting in church a few times just amazed at her beautiful grace. She has a beauty that cannot be defined with words in the physical realm; only my spirit can explain what I am attempting to express. Listening to her speak blessings over her children (the congregation at Redeeming Word) is like pouring water over a plant under the beautiful sun. Her words have a way of increasing peace and confidence in my life and they encourage me, push me, and enlighten me.

She has frequently addressed that she spoke to her teenage son as if he was already in the position as a pastor while he was skipping school, selling drugs, and getting high from narcotics. She spoke blessings over his life while everyone else threw in the towel and gave up on his future. Now she's currently a pastor in Rochester, New York. Her husband, my pastor Apostle Ed Brinson, must be one of the luckiest men on earth. I only get to feed on her words of power once or twice a week but, as her husband, he gets it every day.

That's what marriage and relationships are all about: Encouraging and speaking kind words to each other and over each other. Building each other up!

A man is a lump of coal with a diamond in the middle. It's going to take your words of affirmation, encouragement, and blessings to chip away the dark scars on his heart by applying sweet words to reveal the hidden treasure inside. For a man to transcend from a piece of rock caused by the harsh realities of the world, he is going to need a queen like you to make him see what you see — a king.

The 5 A's Real Men Need:
1) Appreciation

2) Acceptance

3) Admiration

4) Approval

5) Affirmation

A man feels empowered when he is appreciated, accepted, admired, approved, and affirmed. Stroke his ego occasionally, but don't do it so much that it cripples him. Build him up to be a great and powerful king. Encourage him to be an overcomer, a man of God, and the best leader to his ability. Many men feel they were born for greatness, but rarely achieve it to the fullest. That will change now when you give his light a way to shine.

Dear Queen,

Your encouragement is never-ending and creates eternal happiness. As tough as a man may think he is, we all need morale boosting during some point of our lives; a pep talk and cheerleading occasionally, to keep our vision intact.

CHAPTER 6

WOMAN OF FAITH

*Y*ears ago, I had the pleasure of listening to Terri Foye, an inspirational speaker and author from Texas. Mrs. Foye came to my church during a conference to encourage us to believe in our dreams. This beautiful, small-framed, squeaky-voiced White woman blessed us with a powerful message that left a positive impact on our lives, even to this day.

"See with the eye of faith, speak what you see in the spiritual realm until you see it in the natural," she told the audience. "The ideas come first, and the visions come second!"

Her lecture on pulling our ideas into the physical realm was extremely powerful, and it's a lesson I never forgot. I learned that every creative idea manifested started as a thought before it became a reality. I am excited about teaching you how to pull those ideas into the physical realm in the upcoming chapters.

Mrs. Foye taught the congregation about the art of visualizing and seeing the world with your third eye — "eyes of faith." One of the most attractive attributes a woman can bring to the table is her vision and the ability to see beyond the current obstacles to envision the possibilities. Kings throughout ancient history went on vigorous "queen hunting" adventures for women with the gift of clairvoyance, which meant the difference between success for the royal bloodline in the future or the end of the family legacy.

Just because you don't see a way, doesn't mean that God can't make a way!

When your king is going through the battle of his life, or a flat-out war, he will look to you to speak blessings his way. It is not a time to be quiet, passive, or non-supportive. During the battle, he'll listen out for your positive words of affirmation, even when it looks like he has no chance in hell that he'll win. Because, when he loses, you'll lose too. You must remember that it doesn't matter what it looks like with the physical eyes. It's what you say that counts; the words you speak into the universe count. Just because you don't see a way, it doesn't mean that God can't make a way. A queen of faith will speak to her mountains knowing that the DNA of the most-High God has a hedge of protection around her. You know that your family is too blessed to be stressed, and that any challenging situation is only temporary.

Say these words to him the next time you or someone you love bumps into a hurdle: "You are blessed. You are healthy. You are strong. You are talented. You are fantastic. You've bounced back before, and you will bounce back again!"

DNA OF A CHAMPION

When Dodie Osteen, the mother of televangelist Joel Osteen, was diagnosed with liver cancer in 1981, she immediately spoke blessings over her family and herself. Most importantly, she blessed her spirit. News of this magnitude can bring a person to their knees, literally. A mountain like this would have anyone distressed. Your

110

vibrant beating heart will begin to operate at the pace of molasses, but it shouldn't remain that way for someone of faith.

I can see Mrs. Osteen putting up a fist and declaring, "Yes! Whoo-hoo! I can give God a chance to do a bigger miracle."

When she got home after the first report of the cancer, she wasted no time complaining about her situation. Instead, she told her mountain that she was "healed, blessed, and victorious!" She hung up pictures around her home of her happiest moments in life: her children, husband, youthful days, and her closest friends. She had the bounce-back spirit. I'm sure that her husband, John Osteen, was very proud of her and stood tall with her during the process.

Two years later she was as healthy as a lioness with no trace of cancer in her body. Mrs. Osteen knew she had the DNA of a champion — the DNA of an overcomer. We all do, but the only difference is that most of us don't know how to tap into the power of the Creator within us. We're about to change that!

PALM TREE RESILIENCE

Palm Trees: The bounce-back ability. We all have the bounce-back capability rooted deeply in us. The problem is that many of us don't know how to access it. It's like having several million dollars inside a titanium safe but forgetting the combination to unlock it. To make matters worse, let's say it's a recession and your children are starving. You can say you have the combination, but it doesn't mean jack if you don't apply it. It's the same with faith. It doesn't mean a thing if your faith don't have that swing; target your hope on something so it can be activated. That's how you bounce back. What defines us is how well we rise after falling.

A king, let alone your family, doesn't need you walking around claiming to have faith without exhibiting it. Like in any situation, we can say or post anything that looks good on social media, but the proof is in the pudding. Your king is going to fight at least one Goliath while you're together. Even if you have small faith, he'll need to sense it from you. He may very well need your spiritual guidance to tap into the powers of the Creator within you, and you'll need to tap into the grace of God within his heart. Together, you two will be invincible. Remember that our ancestors in Kemet believed they were God in the human form, so don't be so quick to go to the internet for answers when the all-knowing, all-powerful God is within you.

Let hope come alive in you again. When two people are constantly uplifting each other, it's nearly impossible for that relationship to fail. You could presumably be one of those women who know how to use their queendom power to obtain a desired result. Cook a finger-licking meal, stroke your man's ego, and put it on him like it's nobody's business. Many of us are taught about the powers of prayers, sex, and money, but not about the one thing most of us lack — utilizing our power!

ACTIVATE YOUR FAITH

Have you ever heard someone say "I'm in my zone" or "don't kill my vibe"? It's a state of mind that is activated by the melatonin in the pineal gland of our brain. When it's aligned with our thoughts, it creates the goals we seek to make a reality in life. People are usually in the zone during an athletic competition or while working on something important. We have access to this powerful tool, which allows us to focus on what we want to accomplish in life, especially when it comes to the things we have put our faith in. Melatonin is also the key element to accessing the spiritual realm — the seat of the soul, which is the pilot of the body. The pineal gland is also known as the third eye, and the "eye of insight," providing perception beyond our ordinary sight.

"One who does not have a ship cannot cross the river." ~ African Proverb

The ship is the pineal gland, and the river is the melatonin it produces. If you were to include the third eye, a couple joining their eyes and minds together have a total of six eyes. The average person has 200 billion brain cells, and with two people joining forces, that number doubles to 400 billion brain cells. A couple possessing six eyes and over 400 billion brain cells that think alike and envision the same thing equates to tons of power and might, especially with faith in the equation.

Faith is the substance of things hoped for without the evidence of seeing them. In other words, seeing what isn't yet visible. The type of energy you operate under determines your level of faith. The higher your energy and positive thinking, the higher your level of expectation when it comes to faith. There is an energy level chart called the Chakra System, which has seven levels. It's the energy level system of the body. The color green represents the fourth Chakra, which is the heart region of the body. Its characteristic is acceptance, and its principle is compassion for others. The objective of reaching this Chakra level is to think with the intelligence of your heart and to feel with your mind. We're conditioned to think with our mind on every decision, which causes us to ignore our natural instincts.

If we're honest with ourselves, the motto "it's just business; don't take it personally" doesn't really apply to all of us. People take business "to heart" and make it personal. There is no way to detach yourself. Everything you do and what you're passionate about is done with your heart. This is a great attribute for a woman to have if her heart is pure with goodness. Your mind can fly over the coo-coo's nest, but the heart is going to stay put. Your heart can grow cold but not crazy. What's in the heart will come out of the mouth and ultimately become your reality. When purpose (heart), focus (eyes), and intention (spirit) are combined, you have a recipe for a supernatural phenomenon.

"A Grateful Heart Is a Magnet for Miracles!"

HEART POWER

Our heart impacts the decisions we make, which impacts our faith. The good book even tells us in Proverbs 4:23, "Above all else, guard your heart, for it determines the course of your life."

The essence of healing rituals is based on the belief that an exchange of energy occurs to facilitate healing between two people near each other and the "belief" that healing will occur. It's difficult when your heart is heavy and foul on a low level of consciousness or filled with negative thoughts. Revenge, resentment, past hurts, unwillingness to forgive, and hate will manifest itself. You will produce foul energy that will create a horrendous world in your immediate environment and contaminate the poor souls entrapped in your web of negativity.

We need to shift our moods into something positive that will drastically improve our emotions, mentality, and immediate surroundings. Your overall outlook on life will go through a metamorphosis, making you extremely attractive to a potential mate. This shift of consciousness is one of the most powerful and simple tools to which we all have access. We can use this power every day by simply being conscious of the power of words. The spells we cast on people with our words are either blessings or curses we speak into the universe. The root word of spelling is "spell." When people place a spell on another person, it is usually one with words. Be mindful of the words you speak, and the intentions of the words you use.

Furthermore, your appreciation for life will taste like sweet mangos in the summer breeze. Do you realize how much a man needs to feel appreciated by his woman? It means the world to men and increases their desire to experience life as one. Walking in the rain to enjoy every drop together. Jumping in a pool fully clothed together. Watching a movie while indulging in cookies and milk. Enjoying a picnic underneath shade from a huge tree with beautiful green leaves. Taking the time to hug each other for longer periods of time. Appreciating the simple things in life. Together.

Showing your man that you truly care and have faith in his vision gives you an immense amount of influence in your world and his world. Most relationship coaches will tell you to support and love your man unconditionally. I have a different suggestion to offer. Go after his vision because that's where his spirit will be. Your heartbeat will have an upbeat rhythm in sync with his heart, allowing you to ride his energy wave. You will see how positive your world will become together. Choosing to pull his energy and brain cells away from his dreams will only come to bite you in the rear end at the end. Having faith in your gentleman will give him natural encouragement and add more fuel to your passionate love life together.

As a queen, you will have control over the magnetic fields of everything around you. A king's job is to protect you and the things you gave birth to together: children, businesses, and community endeavors.

Do not allow your emotions to dictate your decisions, because your judgment will be tainted. If we're going to get our families in order (with a loving mother and father in the home), women will have to reign as righteous rulers, queens, and women of God. The suppression of women's creative energy has been going on far too long. A king's strength comes from his queen. It's co-rulership.

ASK YOURSELF THESE FOUR QUESTIONS:

1. If your heart was a river, what kind of water would be flowing from it?

2. Would this water sustain life, or would it destroy those around you?

3. Would everyone want to drink from you because you're a well of blessings?

4. Would they choke because of your toxic energy?

Only you know the answers.

LOVE'S REFLECTION

In the Bible, Proverbs 4:20-22 states: "Listen carefully to my words. Don't lose sight of them. Let them penetrate deep into your heart, for they bring life to those who find them, and healing to their whole body."

This scripture shows us that the ancient civilizations knew about the technology of the heart thousands of years ago. Historians believe it was more than a million years ago. Somehow, they knew that the condition of one's heart (their "love life") has an impact on the health of his or her whole body and its reflection of their world. In other words, take care of the heart, and your mind, body, and the soul will be taken care of as well. It's the Nile River of your body. No wonder so many young couples look like they're 60 years old and struggling in life, yet 60-year-old couples are smiling while enjoying their life. They appear as if they're still in their youth. The heart has the power to heal; therefore, it also has the power to make someone heartsick, including the people around them. "The Principle of Polarity" means that there are two sides to everything in life.

What if the frequencies from your brain and heart (electromagnetic) waves could make you a powerful woman in the world? What are you going to use your power for?

One can only hope that you use this power to uplift your family and community. Perking up your man's self-confidence and integrity should be simple. This also goes for your sons, cousins, and fathers — all the males in your sphere of influence. Could you imagine a world filled with "upright men" who felt great about themselves? Imagine the kind of love energy they would emit throughout the streets of the ghettos, suburbs, and Third World countries if millions of men walked around with a high level of confidence. This could create the type of fathers who will stand and fight for the honor of their family's name and the women in their neck of the woods while protecting, providing, and building for their neighborhood. Communities around the world could be turned around if every single person showed everyone around them love and generosity. Love's reflection will take over the world! How can we get to this point? Queens, you are the solution.

CHEMISTRY & ENERGY

With every thought that we create, an electrical pulse flows all over and inside of our temples millions of times per second. Thinking positive thoughts allows our good ideas to manifest, while thinking negative thoughts allows our nightmares to turn into a living reality. A king with a vision needs you to encourage him. Like the Nile River, you are his source of power in the physical realm. A man needs your electrical catalyst to act on his creative ideas. Sure, men can do many good things on our own without the aid of our women; however, we will need the powers of the feminine principle if we want to take our goals to the next level. This was the way of our ancestors, and we need to get back to those traditional ways of life if we want to rebuild our families.

Has anyone ever told you: "We come
up with some great ideas together!"

or

"Every time you come around
I get the best ideas!"

A smart person would try to hang around you as much as possible. Your exchange of energy together in the same time and space ignites powerful ideas. Could you imagine what would happen if you acted upon some of those ideas? If you're spending that valuable time nagging, then you'll have less time for encouragement. Simply turn it around and focus on moving forward. New ideas give us hope. They also give our faith employment.

You'll notice how you repel around some people whenever they come around. The brain operates as an epicenter of information, which controls the body and the surrounding environment. Think of the brain as a supercomputer with thousands of sparks going off simultaneously. It is best to avoid people who will download negativity into your computer system. Choose to surround yourself with those who believe in you and have faith in your vision.

The atoms of faith are always within us, and sometimes it takes a drastic situation to enable faith to grow exponentially. You must give faith a reason to grow beyond paying bus fares, rent, and car notes. If that is all you're praying for, that's all you're going to get. Give your faith employment.

"There is no impossibility to anything." - Flo-Jo

Dear Queen,

Remember that your thoughts create your world. If you think it, you can make it happen.

CHAPTER 7

NATURAL QUEEN

*Beauty is the way you make people feel
and how you feel about yourself. Beauty
is your spirit – it's your soul.*

A natural queen, or a conscious sister, understands her role in nature and life on a global scale. Once upon a time, before all the chemicals, perms, and weaves were so popular with women of African descent, hair was perceived as an antenna. Rastafarians see their dreadlocks as high-tension wires which transmit divine energy and inspiration from Jah (God) the creator. If our body is the temple of God, our hair is the natural crown.

Why would you wear weaves and extensions year-round and hide your crown from the sun? That's like hiding your plants from the sun's nutrients, which need it to grow. Everything about you is part of your feminine beauty. Your look, style, and smile represent your brand.

I know many women will want to throw a shoe at me for saying what I am about to say. As a king, I consider those women who do not groom their short or long hair to be lazy. Hiding behind wigs and weaves 365 days a year is boring and unhealthy. The chemicals that sisters use in their hair are slipping into their bloodstream, which makes it dangerously unwholesome.

I understand that it's often tedious to wash, dry, and manage your hair. Yet, the natural look, feel, and smell of fresh, clean, natural hair is beautiful. It is more attractive and incomparable. If time is a factor, then let's look at what women of the past did in their spare time.

RESOURCEFULNESS

For starters, when it came to natural hair care, the Native Americans reigned supreme due to their beauty secrets and resourcefulness. The leaves from the cactus, called prickly pear, were used as an anti-inflammatory and moisturizer to hydrate their skin for long hours. Saw palmetto was one of the most important beauty secrets because it was a natural hormone regulator and helped women rid themselves of unwanted body hair. Indigenous Americans discovered aloe vera, one of the greatest natural remedies on the planet. The Native Americans were forced to live on reserves that were extremely dry and sandy. All the while, the people used aloe vera as a source of natural and long-lasting hydration. That's what I call being resourceful.

Over time, they ascertained that when sweet grass is boiled and dipped into one's hair within the water, it leaves the hair shiny with a sweet scent. It is also a cure to treat wind-chapped lips. Women used yarrow and witch's broom shampoo to keep their hair continuously looking and smelling good. The Native American's discovery hundreds of years ago caused many shampoo and cosmetic industries to implement their own yucca plantations. This made it possible to keep up with the demands of their customers.

Furthermore, prior to what we now call America, the women of Nez Percé took their time to knit materials together, such as quilts, clothes, and baskets. These projects took weeks and months to create, depending on the size. Native American tribes knit extravagant purses made from bitterroot, camas bulbs, and other roots that were unearthed. They used their creativity to produce different clothing styles and new forms of housing, such as the hide-covered tepees and pit-tepees. Using natural products and their creative energy, they made beautiful bags with strands of Indian hemp and grass, intertwined in geometric patterns.

As they were being forced into reservations by the exploiters of Europe, the women started making the purses smaller and more decorative. Just like today, the purses were made for their own personal use or as gifts. They would not part from them. As one Yakima woman said, "They are too precious."[1] They weaved these bags with canvas and applied grass beads to form colorful designs, many of them featuring floral or animal motifs. It took a week to make these all-natural products. These women learned how to use their creativity and talents to maintain a natural hair care and beauty regimen. It wouldn't hurt to look deeper into their natural beauty recipes; in fact, it may just save your health.

Mane Attraction

The Black hair care industry has made nearly half a trillion dollars a year since 2012, with a projection of $761 million by the end of 2017. In fact, half a billion dollars is spent on weave annually. It pleases me that a natural hair movement has taken place. Your hair should make you feel good and become a part of your beauty. According to Nielsen, African Americans currently hold a buying power of $1 trillion, a number that's estimated to reach $1.3 trillion by 2017. And they're blowing a lot of those bills on cosmetics, spending nine times more on ethnic-targeted beauty and grooming products than the general market. Black women, in particular, spend an estimated $7.5 billion annually on beauty products, shelling out 80% more on cosmetics and twice as much on skin care as their non-Black counterparts."[2]

Now, if a man accepts you wearing weave most of the time, then that's his business. However, what if I told you that the glue used to attach the weave on top of your natural hair has chemicals that cause cancer and permanent hair loss? Ask supermodel Naomi Campbell, who suffered from a condition called *traction alopecia*. It's a form of gradual hair loss that may be caused by certain weave styles, such as: tight ponytails or (micro) braids that pull on sensitive hair roots. The only remedy to this condition is a transplant. This surgical procedure requires removing strong hair roots from your head and transplanting them to the scarred hairline.

In case you're wondering about the cost of the procedure, it comes at the hefty cost of $4,000. That's a drop in a bucket for people like Naomi, but it could take years for the average working woman to save up that kind of money. Most insurance companies won't cover the procedure. This issue isn't only affecting Black women, but it impacts White women as well. Actress Jennifer Aniston complained that she lost hair after using extensions for a prolonged period, which is a method widely used in Hollywood's "show business" to give the stars that glamorous look we are programmed to worship. The only difference between actresses and the "Janes" of the world is that they get paid to wear costumes — you don't! Please stop believing the hype the media is selling you, because it's destroying your natural beauty and health.

It's not uncommon to hear that men prefer their women to wear weave. They are entitled to that, especially if they are dishing out the greenbacks for it at the price of $60-$500 a hairdo. That money can be used to feed a family or to save up for higher education. However, if you inform him of the health risks, and he still persists that you continue to torture your scalp with glue, extensions, and weaves, then you know he doesn't have your best intentions in mind. You're dealing with an insecure man who wants an artificial woman. Every man wants to see his reflection in his woman. In this case, he wants to see a façade — a woman who doesn't exist. When you're making love, he may start fantasizing about being intimate with someone else and not you. It's an illusion, mirage, and fantasy, which creates the perfect ingredients to an unhealthy relationship.

Many men love to play with their woman's natural hair. It's an affectionate way of bonding together. It is kind of hard to complain that you can't find a "real man" when your appearance isn't real. You attract what you project into the universe. It's troubling to see the kinds of fruits that are developed by two fake individuals: girls and boys who grow up to be adults without any comprehension of what it is to be a *real* woman or man. Girls develop into women covering up all their natural beauty with cosmetics, weaves, and plastic surgery. There is so much emphasis on the external beautification, and the most important internal elements that make you truly gorgeous are obscured. I love to see a woman dolled up like the next man, but only to a certain degree. The mind and spirit should never take a back seat.

To be clear, I am not saying that all women who wear weaves, extensions, and acrylic nails aren't good women or queens; nor am I implying they have low self-esteem. Self-image is vitally important on multiple levels, especially when it comes to people of power. It can make or break your whole world. Your system of ideas is based on your self-image, and a poor perception of yourself will result in a poor system of ideas and low self-esteem. The excessive use of cosmetics and poor care of your body results in desecration of your sacred temple.

If a suitable companion desires your friendship, he'll honor your natural beauty. As a king myself, I would. No makeup, no weave, no implants — just the real you. He'll even love your natural sweet morning breath. It's amazing how things grow on us without even noticing it. That's the power of energy. It encompasses everything and everyone around us. Naturally speaking, this gives your relationship an extension of happiness.

SELF-REFLECTION

In many tribal societies, the self-reflecting power of mirrors was believed to have the power of revealing the soul. That is why it is vitally important to look at yourself and embrace images of your life's greatest moments as often as possible. [Do it now!] We all have a few attributes about us. Once upon a time, you experienced an oasis of happiness. Your mind flew free like a bird. Grasp those positive vibrations and use that to reverse those harbored emotional scars due to bad experiences from your past. We all have them — some of us just practiced long enough to tame those emotions. They are tucked away in the darkest crevices of our brain. The mind is a terrible thing to waste, but it's a joy when we use positive thinking as a tool. We may not have full control of what briefly crosses our mind, but we do have complete control over the thoughts we dwell on. Every word we speak is a spirit that creates our individual worlds.

The good news is that those great moments of your past could be replayed again, again, and again! In fact, when you're depressed, think about those great moments, and you'll SNAP OUT OF IT! Besides, it doesn't matter how fine you are ... no man wants a woman who's constantly in sorrow or in some state of depression.

Having a good sense of direction during your life's journey means you're on your way to a wealthy place. If you're able to understand another person's needs and have self-confidence and self-acceptance, then your self-definition will also be enhanced. Who you see in the mirror will be as beautiful as can be. These qualities make you an extremely attractive woman. A man will find you irresistible, especially with stimulating conversations. Some of us prefer intellectual discussions, while others opt in for sexual conservations.

You don't want your soul mate to get with you and then realize that all you can offer is a pretty weave, attractive body, and good sex. If that's the case, he could string you along until another woman comes along who does the same. To increase your chances of securing a good man, I suggest showing him that you can rock his world! This can be done by consistently encouraging him, speaking blessings over him, building a business together, and cooking great meals you can enjoy together. If these things are too much for you, you may end up seeing pictures of him on Instagram or Facebook marrying someone else. You will find yourself thinking that it should have been you, but you got Bobo instead of a Boaz.

Some men will go after an emotionally weak woman, especially if she's attractive. There's a misconception that all men want a trophy wife. We may seek a PYT (pretty young thing), but a good, emotionally strong woman doesn't have to be the prettiest thing on the block. Most young men go for the physical qualities of a woman. However, a mature, wise man who has been seasoned by bad dating experiences and heartaches will want to make one woman his queen when he's ready to settle down. A quality man will go for a woman with a good heart because inner beauty is eternal and not frivolous. It's not uncommon for famous men to marry normal, average-looking women who are considerate, down-to-earth, and comfortable to live with day to day.

YOU ARE THE EPITOME OF BEAUTY

Queens come in all shapes, sizes, colors, and spirits. With the technology and advancement in cosmetics, a woman can turn into Queen Nefertiti or Nicki Minaj overnight. It's amazing how time, money, and energy can improve our lives when we concentrate on our resources. A high self-worth will elevate our lives and those we allow into our world over time.

It's almost as if women are being driven to be discontented with their natural beauty. Some women dislike themselves because they don't have what society considers beautiful: big breasts, a huge wobbling booty, or a gap between their thighs. We have developed a culture of women who must promote their beauty based on what the media wants us to value. Values are accepted behavior by a given culture. We should be concerned that television determines what most of the population considers valuable. The end result is a society of shallow women who weren't taught about the spiritual beauty within themselves as internal goddesses.

It's hard to believe that actress Phylicia Rashad thought she wasn't pretty. Phylicia said that she figured that when God created her, he must have been "on a lunch break."

She mentioned during a 1987 interview with Oprah, "I never thought of myself as beautiful as the other girls. Plus, I thought my legs and neck were too long."[3]

At the age of eleven, she was a great orator at her school and had to memorize a script as the narrator of a musical program for all the elementary schools in Houston, Texas. The event was held in front of a couple thousand people in the audience. The light blinded her when she stepped on stage, and she couldn't see anyone. She could only look into the glaring spotlight and speak toward it.

Phylicia looked deep inside herself without worrying about how anyone looked and gave one of the greatest performances of her young life. She realized her beauty in that moment, and it was a defining moment indeed. Years later, the world fell in love with her humorous, intelligent, and nurturing spirit as Mrs. Huxtable from *The Cosby Show*. She continues to star in many Academy Award-winning movies today. Her mother taught her many important affirmations to give her confidence, such as the following:

"The inner reality creates our outer
form. Look within yourself first!"[3]

Ladies, you are the first art of the world. Your body is a work of art that has captivated men since the beginning of time. Marketing campaigns are built around the beauty of women. Battles have been fought in the honor of women. Nations have been destroyed by wars over women. Some of the world's most beautiful paintings (e.g., the Mona Lisa) have been drawn to admire women in all their natural beauty. You were wonderfully and perfectly made by the Creator. You are a masterpiece designed by God.

Knowing this makes it hard to believe that emergency rooms are filled with women who altered the Creator's design. Unfortunately, some of these butt injections have ended up being fatal. I do understand that many women are aspiring hip-hop and fashion models, singers, or rappers. At the same time, are you willing to risk your life to achieve it? Some silicone injections can end up in your lungs (silicone embolism) and throw off your natural body chemistry.

Case in point, a friend of mine, "Natalia," had to pay a licensed plastic surgeon $7,500 to get corrective surgery on butt silicone injections. She paid $500 to an unlicensed nurse to give her the injections, and it cost her tons of pain. She had to pay out an additional $7,000 a couple of years later. After three years of receiving the injections, she decided to get the surgery done because the pain was too much to endure. She could barely drive or sit at her office desk without discomfort. Many of the women on the *Real Housewives of Atlanta, Real Housewives of New Jersey, Love & Hip Hop*, and other reality television shows have numerous women with fake butts, huge breasts, long synthetic hair, and artificial nails.

Moreover, how can you enhance something that was made perfect? God made you beautiful. You are wonderfully made. Your features are unique and have the power to drive men wild. When your king wakes up in the morning, he will love you for who you are: your morning breath, your messed-up hair, and your natural beautiful makeup-free face.

She's Got that Glow

Have you ever noticed a woman walking around with a pep in her step as if she has a glow about her? We see this when a woman is in a great relationship, or at least has a glimpse of happiness in her relationship. She is reflecting the energy of a good man. He puts that pep in her step. He brings out the best in her and in the most pleasant relationships. The man is simultaneously shining bright. One can look at the old-school saying "one hand washes the other." One's energy elevates the other. He wants you to look and feel great. He needs your energy high for him to reach his own greatness, which is fighting to find a way to manifest.

For the present was once the past, and will become the future.

Your synergy together should create productive endeavors, such as starting a lucrative business, building a home, creating inventions, etc. I personally refuse to be with a woman who cannot absorb my creative energy. Between my books, speaking engagements, and marketing company — my mind is always thinking. I'm continuously planning, and having a woman who can reflect my energy will only increase my positive vibrations. It will bring us closer. A king knows that whenever a woman's touch is involved the visualization becomes a manifestation.

Ladies, when you can't seem to progress things with a gentleman, or there is always an excuse or a reason why he doesn't want to do anything with or for you, it's for one of two reasons: 1) his consciousness level is too low and he doesn't have enough energy to pour into your fountain, or 2) he's just not that into you. Either way, it's your sign to keep it moving. You don't have to read the stars to see that. Both of you are hindering each other's progress.

I've noticed that when a young woman doesn't have a good man in her life, she becomes a dimmed light, stagnant, confused, somewhat disorientated. She searches to find something to invest her positive energy in. She might spend an excessive amount of time worshipping in church, fervently serving in the name of Jesus, or constantly traveling from city to city — all the while acting as if she is so happy and there is no need for a man.

Nevertheless, allow me to introduce you to a "conflict of energy." Unlike the sun and the moon, the true power and energy of a woman are seen on her surface. However, her beauty is felt from within her heart, which is her crown. As the sun rules the day, the moon rules the night, which gives life a perfect balance. The moonlight is simply the reflection of the sun's energy. The glow of a woman is heightened when she is in a relationship with a brilliant, powerful, strong, and disciplined man to support her. It's easy for a man to get caught up in his work and neglect the fact that his supporters need his support too.

You are the crown.

LAW OF REFLECTION

I went to a good friend's exclusive wedding at a five-star resort in Orlando in 2014. The DJ requested that all the married couples get on the dance floor and slow dance. He played a game by calling out the number of years the couples were married, and if they weren't married beyond that amount of time, such as 10 years, they had to sit down.

The DJ went from ten years to twenty years, eventually making his way up to fifty years. The winning couple was married for an unbelievable fifty-seven years!!! The lovely couple received a standing ovation for being married for so long. One can only imagine the struggles and joys these two experienced in their lifetime together. They had to put aside petty arguments and come to an understanding a long time ago: "I got your back and you got mine, forever!"

It's a blessing to look into the mirror with pride of who you've become, not because of the value of your clothes or outer beauty. You can look at yourself, your companion, and see treasure. Looking at your companion without seeing your reflection is like looking into the mirror and not being able to see anything. It's creepy and unnatural.

Understanding the natural "law of reflection" will help us tremendously when it comes to evaluating the quality, strength, and future of our relationships. The law of reflection is the most difficult law for people to accept because we like to think that issues are everyone else's fault but our own.

Choose your mirror wisely, because our partners are really an extension of ourselves. Every person and every circumstance in your life provide you with an opportunity to learn something about yourself. This enables us to better ourselves. Our companions are our mirrors. When we hurt, our partner (and loved ones) is hurting as well. The same can be said if we take care of our partner by honoring and loving on them; then, we honor and love ourselves. In a healthy relationship, the love we project will come back to you tenfold. Moreover, it is for this simple reason that relationships last for over fifty years when partners put the other person before themselves. What we give out is what we get as a reflection of ourselves.

Once you can see this reflection, then you're able to capture the rhythm of your partner.

BE GENUINE. BE YOU.

Understanding your purpose in life makes a world of difference. Fulfilling your purpose while being genuine makes the victories even more special. Embracing your natural beauty and the plethora of blessings that Mother Earth provides will empower you to reduce the usage of cosmetics.

Meanwhile, increase the application of natural beauty products on the market. Learn more about the natural beauty secrets that indigenous societies of the past and present used, as well as your grandparents. This will keep your culture alive for generations to come. Remember, the more conscious you are about your natural beauty, the less likely you'll depend on outside sources to validate your self-beauty. Be the kind of beauty that is hard-to-get and comes from within. Take time to cultivate strength, courage, and dignity. You are beautifully and wonderfully made!

Dear Queen,

A natural woman understands nature, life, and her role in it on a global scale. She's conscious of her environment and the importance of healthy eating and natural beauty.

CHAPTER 8

SEXY QUEEN

"Knowing her is to touch her without
touching her, really touches her."

-Anonymous Author

Every woman has sexy features. Every woman is beautiful. Every woman has energy that possesses its own unique flavor, vibration, and authenticity.

What skills and talents make you different from the next woman? Men are visual creatures, so we are paying close attention to every detail of your wardrobe when you think we are not. Maybe it's a certain type of dress that you wear or a meal that you cook exceptionally well that makes your man's liver quiver. Use it to your advantage in securing your king, but don't let it be the end-all. Many guys are philanderers just looking for a woman to play wifey, but they have no intention of marrying her.

Show him how much more your intelligence and skillset will greatly benefit him and the empire you two will build together. A man with vision will find this aspect about you attractive. The family you create together will become the army that plays different positions in your world, but it's up to you as the queen to set the throne's tone to move your family's legacy forward. Your king will oversee maintaining security to keep peace in the home. It's critical that you choose to crown a man who has your security in mind, and one who's not into you solely based on your sexiness.

A girl will play games with her man's mind.
A Queen will explore it.

In other words, show him how much of a fool he would be not to court you. Show a man who has proven himself that he is worthy of your benefits: time, cooking, hugs, money, and energy. Reveal to him that you can hold a conversation outside of sex, cooking, and fun.

The best way to up your stock is indulging yourself with books and videos on empowerment, finances, and/or science. Listen attentively and observe his hobbies to find out his interests. Act as if you're interested, even if you're not. Grab a book on a subject you both have interest in at least twice a year; you both will gain a lifetime of knowledge. When you research his interests and throw some knowledge at him, he will find you even more attractive. Your conversations together will become revitalizing because you'll be able to stimulate each other's brain cells. Intellectual orgasms occur when two or more people are having deep conversations. Your brain is the largest sexual organ you have. Your mind should be the sexiest thing about you.

WHAT TO WEAR

Two young ladies showed up to a meeting wearing clothes that were quite revealing. The chairman took a good look at them and asked them to sit down. Then, he looked them straight in the eyes and said something they may not ever forget.

"Ladies, everything that God made valuable in this world is well-covered and hard to see, find, or get. Your body is sacred and unique. You are far more precious than gold, diamonds, and pearls. You should be covered, too. If you keep your treasured jewels just like a precious gemstone — deeply covered up — a reputable mining organization with the requisite machinery will fly down and conduct years of extensive exploration.[1]

"First, they (king) will contact your government (family), sign professional contracts (wedding), and mine you professionally (legal marriage)," he continued. "But if you leave your precious jewels uncovered on the surface of the earth, you will always attract a lot of illegal miners to come and mine you illegally. Everyone will pick up crude instruments and dig on you freely. Keep your bodies covered so that it will invite real suitors to pursue you."

How are you packaging yourself? Are you dressed modestly, or are you a distraction? The way you package yourself determines who will approach you. If you dress too sexy, it will cause horn dogs to approach you more frequently. Dress conservatively, and you'll have more conservative men approach you. Dress like a queen and you will attract kings. Dress like a hoe, and you'll have all types of hoes coming at you, including other women.

THE UNFORGETTABLE STORY OF SARAH 'SAARTJIE' BAARTMAN

Sarah 'Saartjie' Baartman was born in the Gamtoos Valley of South Africa in 1789. Saartjie was an African woman with one of the most voluptuous bodies of her time — super thick! Even her vagina's posterior muscles had men and women in awe, especially European men. The fact that she had an extended labia minora made non-African people (mostly Europeans) view her as a wild or savage female. These perceptions were due to racism, as a social system to portray African women's unique and beautiful features as ugly.

At the age of twenty-one, she was coerced by a British surgeon in 1810. They wanted her to go into Europe, a foreign land far from her homeland of Khoikhoi in the southwestern region Africa. With the pretense of making money to support her family, she agreed to have her body studied, not realizing they would hold her against her will for years to come. She was enslaved and displayed as a freak show exhibit and endured multiple cruel experiments. They held Sarah in cages and forced her to spend years in London dancing naked in front of crowds — both day and night.

A person could view Sarah's body for the price of two shillings; and for an extra shilling, they touched or poked her anywhere on her body. Degenerates lined up to take advantage of the opportunity; they looked under her protruding skirt (if she had one on), and rubbed on her private parts. Every day from 1 pm to 5 pm, men and women came to stare at and admire Sarah at the freak show. In London Town, they brought her to a theater in a cage and placed her on a stage, three feet from the floor. She was told to act like an animal. When she didn't want to come out of the cage, she was slapped and hit with a bamboo stick while the crowd laughed, spilled their wine and beer over one another, and pointed at her.

This had to be a completely humiliating experience for her. The level of degradation cannot be put into words. This incident caused such an uproar that abolitionists caught wind of it from around the world. The African Association, the equivalent of a charity or pressure group, conducted a newspaper campaign for her release. [Similar to the #BringOurGirlsBack social media campaign for the two hundred girls kidnapped in Nigeria on April 14, 2014. Many honorable women, including First Lady Michelle Obama, supported the movement to bring the girls back safely. Only a couple of them have been able to escape. Please, keep them in your prayers.]

The Anti-Slavery League and the International African Institute in London took up Sarah's case to fight for her freedom. They released a series of articles to the press about the horror Sarah Baartmaan experienced in the United Kingdom. There was a public outcry at this travesty. Brainwashed by the abuse and dependency, Sarah told the King's Bench, the highest civil court in 1810, that she chose to perform in her shows and didn't want to return to South Africa. Therefore, the court dismissed the complaint.

Once Sarah was freed in France, she eventually sought ways to make ends meet. As a foreigner in France without a job, food, education, shelter, or help from family or friends, she ultimately turned to selling her body, temple, and soul in the red-light district as a way of making a living.

Men took her, praised her, used her, and then threw her away when there was no more use for her. Sounds pretty much like what is going on in our society today. Sarah, like many women, was so used to being worshiped physically, and when the praise for her physical body died down, her reason for being died too.

On December 29, 1815, Sarah died at the age of 26. Even in death, she had no peace. A French museum took her body and kept her skeleton as an exhibit. They looked at her as an exotic anomaly. Upon her death, Sarah's body was shipped to George Cuvier's laboratory at the Museum of Natural History for examination. Curvier wanted to examine her genitals to test his racist theories in the name of science. He believed that the more "primitive" the mammal, the more pronounced the sexual organs and sex drive of an African woman. Sarah refused to partake in his experiment while alive. With the permission from the French authorities, Cuvier conducted an autopsy of Sarah's body. He made a cast of her body and then preserved her brain and genitals.[2]

During 1814-1870, it must be mentioned that Cuvier dissected several other African women, whom he called the "Hottentots" or, sometimes, "Bush women." He viewed the so-called "savage woman" as very distinct from the "civilized females" of Europe. Sarah, also known as the "Hottentots Venus," fascinated the nineteenth century science community.

The ignorant people of that time were right about one thing: people of African descent were — and still are — very distinct because they are descendants of a royal bloodline — queens and kings of the world's first high culture civilizations. Through social engineering, many women of African descent are led to think of themselves as less than worthy. They have no idea that African women set the standards and trends of physical beauty as manifested in feminine physique, creative hairstyles, cosmetics, and fashions.

Sarah's body was finally brought back to Khoisan in 1996 to rest in peace. Today, women are consciously selling and exhibiting their bodies for attention, fame, and fortune. The only difference is that women today are free to make all decisions regarding their body, as they are not forced like Sarah "Hottentots Venus" Baartmaan.

GATEWAY

Women are feminine, magnetic, and soft by nature. They are made to receive the man's energy. A woman in tune with her essence uses gentle persuasion and a soft approach to impose her will. Her sexual organs are all located inside the body while men's sexual organs are outside the body. The act of sex has always been the most sacred act in which one man and one woman can partake. Intercourse is the only natural way to procreate. Our ancestors knew the opening of a gateway was possible through powerful lovemaking, otherwise known as "worship sessions." This gateway could manifest the unseen world into the seen, real world. In layman's terms, powerful, backbreaking, connecting sex was used to open a portal or bridge from the spiritual dimension to the physical world during the midnight hours.

"As a woman, you are fully responsible for what enters and exits your gateway."

A female's womb has the power to receive the male's energy and decipher his intentions. A woman's intuition is her most powerful gift, but you can only tap into this gift if you are conscious of it. The issue here is that you cannot, and will not, access your destiny as a goddess without the male counterpart who holds the key to your gateway. This is the love energy of your king's mind, spirit, and penis.

Now, don't get it twisted. Just because a man sticks his energy into a woman doesn't mean there's going to be a beautiful creation coming out of her gateway. You can look at the juvenile detention centers and prisons to see the results of misguided energy. What was meant to be a blessed life turns out to be a malediction.

For the most part, when two people with troubled lives have intercourse and conceive a child, they open a "gateway" or "doorway" to hell on earth. In many cases, those troubled parents came from a long bloodline of negative spirits. It's going to take a woman or man within that family, who possesses a strong faith in God, to break the generational curse. By knowing and exhibiting that you are a child of the most-high God, the Creator, you will find true power and wealth. There is nothing sexier than a woman of faith.

FLO-JO: THE SPEED OF BEAUTY

One of the most electrifying athletes to grace the sports world went by the name "Flo-Jo." Florence "Flo-Jo" Delorez Griffith was one of the most beautiful women in the world and just happened to be an Olympic track and field star. Flo-Jo ate extremely healthy and worked hard to promote healthier diets. She once said the following in a 1997 *JET* magazine interview:

"Health and fitness should be a part of everyone's life. When we take good care of our bodies, our bodies take good care of us in return. Eating right and exercising has been scientifically proven to help prevent certain disease and promotes longer and healthier lives."[3]

Moreover, Flo-Jo shocked the Olympic trial audience at a track meet by wearing a purple bodysuit with turquoise bikini briefs over it, and nothing on her left leg. She dazzled the world as a fashion designer and created her own uniforms, such as the popular "one-leg" tracksuit. To her credit, when Flo-Jo retired from track, she designed the 1989 Indiana Pacers' uniform. In 1993, former President Bill Clinton named her co-chair of the President's Council on Physical Fitness, an extremely high honor.

Flo-Jo might've started her life in the Jordan Downs projects in Los Angeles, California, but she came so far, like a shooting star. She proved you don't have to remain in the ghetto if you focus your energy outside of the ghetto. Currently, there are thousands of little girls in the hoods of America. As a grown woman and Mother God — it's your duty to show them a way out! (Each one must reach one — pay it forward!

Flo-Jo passed away in 1998 from a seizure in her peaceful sleep, but before she flew away to heaven, she gave back to her community in a major way! Flo-Jo made sure that thousands of kids growing up in devastated homes and government housing believed in themselves as she did. Her purpose was to help children make the best use of their talents.

Before there was Flo-Jo, Wilma Rudolph inspired tons of little girls. This includes Flo-Jo, whom would become the superstar that kicked the Olympic doors wide open. Ms. Rudolph reigned on and off the track in the 1960s. As a Black woman, she understood Flo-Jo looked up to her and returned the compliment, saying: "For a long time, we've been thought of as 'jocks.' Florence brings in the glamour!"

Flo-Jo crowned her king, her husband and former coach, Al Joyner, because he believed in her and supported her dreams. The delightful couple exchanged vows in 1987. Al wouldn't have seen the greatness in her if she didn't believe in herself first! Her husband wasn't a chump by far. He was the 1984 Olympic triple jump champion. They gave birth to a beautiful baby girl, Mary Ruth Joyner, on November 15, 1990. Flo-Jo chose a man who had enough energy to sustain her, uplift her, and help her achieve all the possibilities she saw within herself.

Can you see the benefits of a loving relationship such as theirs? It's the kind of love that keeps getting higher and higher. It's limitless love. I'm sure everything wasn't always peaches and cream, but I'll bet my bottom dollar that there was a lot more uplifting going on than cutting each other down.

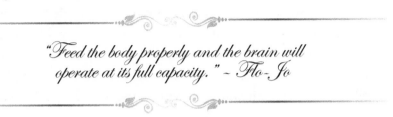

"Feed the body properly and the brain will operate at its full capacity." ~ Flo-Jo

SEXUAL ENERGY

If a man approaches you and starts talking about having sex with you, then he has a low level of consciousness. He's clearly after one thing, so give him an exit. He can hop away like a frog. His only goal is to fulfill the urges of his animalistic nature, which is to survive and procreate. Be warned of this type of male. All he will do is get you pregnant with a lifetime of stress.

When people have one-night stands or seasonal flings, it's considered a low-level of consciousness because it's to satisfy the flesh and not to edify each other. What is supposed to be sacred has turned into a recreational act; it's no different to them than having a meal. The spirit of sex is so powerful that it has turned many lost souls into sex addicts, nymphos. Each act of sex creates a child, a spirit, or both because it is a creation activity.[4]

Dr. Llaila Afrika, author of *Melanin;* and Dr. Frances Cress Welsing, author of *Isis Papers*, explain in their books that we have been brainwashed by mainstream television and the media to believe we have a sex drive.[4] The sex drive is a culturally taught physical behavior (inspired by sexually explicit movies, computer games, music videos, clothes, books, songs, etc.). As humans, we have a reproductive (procreation) drive.

The penis of a man is now a drug to a woman. A woman will find it difficult to eat, sleep, or live a productive life because of the opened door to sexual demons. These are constantly making her horny to the point where she is going mad and only returns to normal after getting a dose of sex. An unhealthy soul tie has been created, and it will take a great amount of effort to sever this bond. Her powers will now be misdirected because of the false king or male who defiled her sacred chamber, womb, and treasure trove, by planting evil seeds in her spirit and body with his penis and negative energy.

GUARD YOUR PEACE OF MIND

You must believe you are a treasure chest filled with good surprises. What we put out into the universe is what we get back. This is known as "the principle of correspondence." I'm not condemning or judging anyone who has had a one night stand or a fling, but the problem I do have with this equation is that children are born as a result.

Ladies, when a man is trying to show you that he is the man for you, take the time, energy, and prayers to open your spiritual eyes to a higher level of consciousness to observe not only his intentions, but also the energy he is projecting. Does he have the STAR POWER to sustain you, uplift you, and handle your energy — Inner-G: the God in you? The answer to this question will tell you if he is worth the headache or drama he could potentially bring into your happy world.

All relationships bring a certain level of headaches into our lives. It's a matter of making a wise decision. Treat your space like it's Fort Knox. Do not let anyone in who doesn't deserve to be. Make your king EARN the right to be in your treasure chest, which is your mind! The valuable aspect about anyone isn't ever their monetary wealth or possessions. It's one's mind. Stop throwing away your gems as if they were disposable. Your peace of mind is at stake.

Your treasure and your temple are sacred. Letting a man into your throne is a blessing. Don't let any man degrade you, belittle you, or disrespect you at will. If he doesn't appreciate what you bring to the table, then he doesn't deserve your treasure.

There are guys who will try to impregnate a good woman with a lot of great things going for herself or a fine woman, because they believe her genes will ensure good-looking children. It sounds primitive; however, it's very common. If you have a good job, house, car, and benefits, a hyena can smell and see you a mile away. Test him to avoid a lengthy relationship with him. Don't give your trust away freely. Allow a man to earn your trust slowly. Step by step in person. Not text by text.

A man should feel honored to be in your presence and flattered that you think about him and want to be seen with him in public. After all, you are giving him your precious energy when you could be spending it with someone else. You're in high demand. You are a queen. Internalize that!

How can you gain all this honor and prestige? You do it by carrying yourself with high esteem and guarding your reputation. Find a positive woman you want to be on par with. They will show you how to dress appropriately and in a classy manner. There is no need to have your breasts bulging out of your dress, your vagina print showing through those yoga tights, or your skirt hiked way above your knees with the bottom of your assets hanging out. There is a huge difference between classy and assy. Even though a man may act and talk about being a gentleman, he'll be thinking about getting in your drawers a large percent of the time. Some guys are walking penises with only sex on their mind. The sexier you dress, the more guys will bark at you. Seriously. You are to discern what type of spirit your suitor operates in. Is it a lustful spirit or a loving spirit with the intention of building a future with you?

Despite the negative image that women, specifically Black women, portray on reality television shows in recent years, these women hold a very powerful position. The power of television goes back into civilizations of antiquity — imagery. Their words and actions travel throughout the airwaves of national television, and internationally via the internet. These, in turn, travel into the psyche of children and adults.

I wish they would use their influence to give girls (in elementary, middle, and high school) better images of what they can accomplish by focusing their energy toward being an entrepreneur, a conscious person, or even a good mother and wife. These women (and men) on reality shows are getting paid one hundred thousand to one million dollars to act like buffoons, while looking fabulous in all their fancy weaves and latest fashions. Money can get us many things, but it cannot buy class.

Symbol of Wealth & Power: Pearls "The Queen of Gems"

Before the creation of cultured pearls in the early 1900s, natural pearls were so rare and expensive that they were reserved almost exclusively for the noble and wealthy. At the height of the Roman Empire, when pearl fever reached its climax, the historian Suetonius wrote that the Roman general Vitellius financed an entire military campaign by selling just one of his mother's pearl earrings.[5]

Natural pearls were once considered one of the most valuable natural objects on earth. They were so sought after, rare, and expensive that Julius Caesar barred women below a certain rank from even wearing them. The face value of a pearl necklace was considered higher than any other piece of jewelry in the world. The ancients believed the pearl symbolized the moon, and women who wore them had magical powers because Mother Nature created them. Men carried them in a sac for the powers they possessed.

When I worked for a Zales jewelry store during college, I learned so much about diamonds, gold, and pearls. Men came in and spent hundreds of thousands of dollars on all sorts of jewelry for their wives, girlfriends, and mistresses. It's almost as if pearls can take a woman's elegance and grace to a higher level — but just like everything else, you can't buy class. If you want to impress people at a formal function without saying much, wear a strand of pearls.

Over time, pearls were embedded in crowns, gowns, necklaces, rings, horse collars, and even cups as a sign of regality. I know there aren't too many women who wear pearls today, but they were worn exclusively by prominent women throughout history. Pearls signify a certain taste in your appearance and a touch of class that is nearly extinct.

THE TOTAL PACKAGE

People often believe that a woman's physical features, including outer beauty, elegance, and sexuality, are most important. All of these traits make her desirable and seductive, but I personally believe a woman's spirit of servitude to her family and community makes her beautiful.

Beauty is in the eye of the beholder.

What one man sees as ugly or unattractive, another man will find beautiful. There are unique features about you, and the right man will appreciate every one of them. The most beautiful woman in the world with the total package — let's say with a Serena Williams body and a Julia Roberts smile — will turn most men off if she has a snobbish attitude, unless he is only around for desperate pleasure. However, a woman with an average body and face and a great attitude isn't considered beautiful, according to the media and society's standards.

It's your benevolent spirit and attitude that enthralls good men of quality — kings! We are drawn to a woman who expects a lot out of life.

JOSEPHINE BAKER: THE BLACK PEARL
"La Perle Noire"

A prime example of a highly spirited woman is American-born French dancer Josephine Baker (born in 1906). She grew up in the slums of East St. Louis, one of the worst ghettos in America during the early 1900s. However, that didn't derail her dreams because her eyes were on the stars above. Josephine was a dreamer. She knew having the right attitude was crucial to reaching her destiny. Being derailed by discrimination, poverty, and other barriers was not an option for her.

Instead of strolling on rose petals as a child, she began her life walking on broken bottles and cigarette butts. Faced with a hopeless situation, she eventually turned it all around by creating her own fantasy world of lights. Camera. Josephine! She was ready to rule and reign!

Ms. Baker resided in her fanciful notion as if it was real, making her fantasy world bigger than her reality. She wanted to be a grandeur dancer all her life, but growing up as a poor girl in the ghetto placed a shade over her dreams. A fantasy world is a lot more fun than the burdens of the ghetto any day. Most people are okay with a mediocre life. They don't have the consciousness to create such a world — it's too risky to them. As the queen of your throne, what mediocre people say shouldn't matter one bit.

Josephine realized one important thing: people enjoy being around others who possess a fiery spirit to make things happen. Keep in mind that the lot you received in life is not the role you should accept for the rest of your life. You can live out a role of your own creation, a role that fits your fancy — your desired reality.

While other people moaned and complained, Josephine smiled. She remained confident and self-reliant. She accepted an invitation to go to France and never looked back, while other African-American dancers declined in fear of being treated worse than the injustices Blacks endured in America during the 1920s and 1930s. The city of love gave Josephine the platform her spirit yearned for all her God-given life. She seized the opportunity. Success is being prepared for an opportunity when it presents itself.

It was time for Lights, Camera, Josephine! She had the boldness of a lioness that was so seductive. She left the French crowds spell-bound and in complete awe! She was more than eye-candy. Josephine was marvelous, hungry for more, and focused on making the best of an opportunity far away from home. These are the perfect ingredients for an overcomer on the come up. Josephine dazzled the crowds, confidently baring her succulent breasts. She demanded that her contracts include a non-discrimination clause. If that wasn't enough, she had the boldness to refuse to perform in segregated clubs in the United States.

Josephine was one of the highest-paid performers in Europe, bringing in a whopping $250 a week (more than double the amount she received in New York while dancing for the Chocolate Danies at the Cotton Club and the Plantation Club in Harlem).

Josephine starred in the "La Revue Nègre," which became a popular three-month jazz show amongst artists and left-intellectuals, such as painter Pablo Picasso and writer Ernest Hemingway in 1927. At the grand opening of the "La Revue Nègre," she wore her graceful birthday suit — a skirt made from a string holding rubber bananas. Responsible for introducing American jazz to France, Josephine earned the title "The Priestess of Jazz." The "Black Pearl," "Bronze Venus" and even the "Creole Goddess" were some of the illustrious names given to her in Europe. Being the highly desirable queen that she was, Queen Baker married three times and divorced three times. I personally don't think the men in her life could handle a woman with such a fiery spirit as hers.[6]

During the years of German occupation in Belgium, Ms. Baker became a Red Cross nurse, watching over the refugees forced to flee their own countries. And when the Germans occupied France, she found a way to help fight against the invaders by joining the French Resistance (a secret army fighting against the occupying German forces) as an underground courier. She later received the Croix de guerre from the French military, which is equivalent to the American Medal of Honor.

The later years of Josephine's life were dedicated to fighting segregation and racism in the United States. When she passed away on April 12, 1975, she was buried with military honors and crowned "The Eiffel Tower of the Music Hall." More than 20,000 people lined the streets of Paris to witness her burial, and the French government was generous enough to bury her with a 21-gun salute, honoring her as the first American woman in world history to be buried in France with military honors.

Josephine turned from a teenage dreamer picking food out of garbage bins in alleys to a world-renowned game changer. Josephine

Baker made a name for herself by changing her birth name, Freda Josephine McDonald, from nothing to something.

Before she went to heaven, Josephine Baker's name became a brand with a line of perfumes, dolls, and clothes. Fashionable French women slicked their hair back a la Baker, using the Baker fix, a product named in her honor. Ms. Baker's name became a franchise in Europe; some even tried to darken their skin to look like her. Josephine had all of France in love with her exoticness; the sister was fine as all outdoors. She knew that distinguishing herself from the stigma created about African American women and every other entertainer in Paris was the only way she would make it. The world was hers for the taking, and she knew it! Ms. Baker took the country by storm and became the heart of France!

MIND STIMULATION

We are constantly controlling and manipulating our body and surrounding atmosphere, whether we know it or not. Josephine Baker, Oprah Winfrey, Marilyn Monroe, and countless other great women in history created their path out of the ghettos and trailer parks into a life of success and substance for themselves and their communities. As a queen, it's vitally important to create the empire you desire. Create a supporting staff to make your life the star of the show! Of course, you can also support your staff in every way possible. Don't be selfish. One hand washes the other.

As far as wifey material goes, yes, you want to be sexy. But there is a difference between sexy and trashy. It's great to be extremely attractive and great in bed, but it isn't everything. It will take a lot more than sex to keep a great man.

153

For instance: Amber Rose, a goddess hands down, is probably one of the finest celebrity Millennial women to date on television. However, things didn't work out for both Kanye West and Wiz Khalifa. This proves you need to have more than a bombshell body to keep a man. Sex isn't everything, and neither are looks. Your mind and consciousness mean the world.

There's an old saying that when you meet a woman with more books than pairs of shoes, she's a keeper. However, if she has more shoes than books, then she shouldn't be introduced to Momma because she may lack intellectual substance to maintain a conversation, let alone a marriage. I don't agree with that old saying, but I see why some people feel this way.

It's a great thing to turn off your television, phone, and other devices at times! Invest more time in developing your mind, body, and spirit. The mind of a goddess is like a galaxy filled with bright stars — whatever you place your mind and energy on will appear over time. Aim to stimulate his mind beyond your sexy pillow talk and curves and will him to you, because now you're having intercourse with his brain (that's four hundred billion brain cells intermingling). Once we have a physical orgasm or two, it's over, but mind sex lasts all day. The physical realm is limited, and the spiritual plane is infinite.

You have the power to control this aspect of your life, so do it! Give yourself an opportunity to be a superwoman and stay in tune with yourself and your world. Be the goddess you are.

TAKE CARE OF YOUR TEMPLE

Sleep deprivation is the number one reason so many women walk around cranky. With our busy schedules and millions of distractions, it's hard to find time to enjoy relaxation, meditation, and good deep sleep. Having a man in the home should help you buy more time to get the peaceful rest your body deserves.

It's been proven that sleep gives our brain an opportunity to do some housekeeping by flushing out the toxic molecules built up in our brain during waking hours. That is why we feel more energetic and in a better mood when we wake up from a great night's rest. Feed your spirit with good sleep and deep prayer meditations so that you can reach higher levels of consciousness. This allows you to find intellectual solutions to problems that riddle you and your loved ones.

Maybe you used to work out three times a week, and now you barely exercise three times a year. Your man is expecting that same bombshell body you had when you first met. It may seem unrealistic, but try to take care of your body. Find a health and exercise system that works for you — don't let your body go with the wind. The last time I checked, being sexy did not go out of style. We all have the power to create time for what we are passionate about.

Don't just let your body go because you have kids or you're getting older. You need to bring those fireworks back into your relationship, even if it's just a little spark. Get your sexy back! You're a woman, so it isn't too hard because you were born to be attractive. It isn't fair to take all the time in the world to get dolled up for work, church, and a ladies' night out, but you put on whatever when it comes to your man. Take the time to put on something sexy. Sometimes men need a reminder of why they chose you and blocked out the flock of women pursuing them. Let's face it; some men need those extra reminders. Wear a nice dress and a cute hairdo just for him, and stay home. Hide the hair rollers and oversized T-shirts. Make him want to give you his energy naturally.

MOVE TO YOUR OWN RHYTHM DAILY

You must control your own rhythm to maintain and increase your power in life. The beat you move to during the day and night must be created by you, or you'll be skipping on hot coals whenever people who control your rhythm decide to push your buttons (e.g., bill collectors, landlords, abusive companions, ungrateful relatives, etc.). People in control of their own rhythms are happy, stable, and a pleasure to be around. You'll be able to recognize them because they don't complain much, and they rarely rush throughout life. Their aura is like a gust of fresh cool wind on a hot summer day. Being in their presence is a blessing.

THE STEPS TO CONTROL YOUR RHYTHM & INCREASE YOUR VIBRATIONS

1) Give the Creator thanks at every sunrise. Say a prayer in the morning when you wake up, and say something positive to yourself or to your spouse. As you close your eyes, think about how the sun's rays are blessing the world with light. If it's possible, go outside on your balcony or yard to let some of the sun touch your skin (while praying or meditating).

2) Listen to gospel, classical, or smooth jazz music in the morning. Choose something positive, edifying, and relaxing. Refrain from watching the news once or twice a week, and then stop watching it altogether if possible. See how it feels. There is too much negativity on the news, and it will disrupt your focus. A drop of bad news can seep into you and place you into a slight depressive state. The goal is to keep you at a high level of vibrational energy.

3) Do not open your bills as soon as you see them. As a matter of fact, hide them from your plain view for a couple of days, and don't think about them. When you get up in the morning, don't look at your phone, unless it's to turn off the alarm or check the time.

4) Light some incense and open a door/window to hear Mother Nature's tune. If you can't do this without hearing loud noises, then it's time to put your energy into finding a new, more peaceful place to lay your head. Your finances may not be where you want them right now, but take what you've learned in this book and speak your dreams and goals into existence. There's a lot more in store for you.

5) Get the proper amount of sunlight daily because it's healthy food for the body and soul. After praying for a few minutes, or however long you deem fit, think about something positive you want to happen to you or someone you love. It's crucial that you don't answer any calls, emails, or send any text messages during this process. The purpose of controlling your rhythm is to continually build up your energy and to block others from attempting to tear you down.

Once you've set the rhythm for your day, you are now prepared to deal with the world in a much calmer state. Now, *you* have the power to control the tempo of your life.

"Dreams do come true. Get away from dream killers. Keep praying, keep being happy, keep striving, and keep believing!"

YOUR LOVE SHOW

We become what we water with our energy and infuse with our faith the most. If you continue to entertain the wrong energy with your time and sacred bodily fluids, many of your dreams will fly right over your head. Instead of watering your dream, you'll find yourself feeding your nightmares. We have the power to speak our dreams until we see them before our very eyes. If you are not being fed the right physical and spiritual energy, you will not reach your fullest potential (i.e., what God called you to do on earth).

In the movie *Coming to America*, Lisa McDowell (played by Shari Headley), spoke words that Eddie Murphy's character (Prince Akeem Joffer), traveled across the globe to hear. Ms. McDowell's intelligence, infectious smile, and love for her community made her sexy. She was involved with a man who had a low level of consciousness, but she ended up with a king. There is so much more to a man than his bank account. There are many other things to consider. Go after a man's money, and you will get it. Find your way into his heart, and you'll get his heart and his money — the empire.

Every man is a headache to some degree, but which one is worth it? Which one is worth your honey lips? Which man deserves to become your crowned husband? I hope this book clears up any confusion that you've had about your importance.

Any practical person understands that we live in a very selfish and harsh world. In this cruel world, little girls witness abuse or are directly abused. This makes them vulnerable. You may feel unworthy of love. This makes it harder for you to determine your worth, especially with the trash being pumped into our psyches 1,000 times a day through our phone, TV, and computer screens.

Create your own vision. Turn your mental channel into your own Love Show, hosted by you! Deep within your subconscious mind, the feeling of worthlessness generates the fear of needing others. A part of you may feel as if you will not be supported. Ironically, men are primarily motivated by being needed, but overtly needy women turn them off. It sucks extra energy out of us.

I've met, dated, and befriended a few women with a tremendous amount of potential. They had the energy to become some of the most accomplished people on earth. However, they mixed their energies and vibrations with too many wrong men who inculcated their lives with toxic vibes. These men have left them with hurt spirits, completely changing their rhythm to lower frequencies and expectations out of life. This keeps people focused on the past and not the present and the future. Your mind and spirit will need a tune-up to maintain higher frequencies to focus on present experiences, conveying what is happening where you are right now in life. Consistent positive energy from those around you invites higher vibrations, adding to your sexiness.

KINGDOM WITHIN YOU

For a man to become a king, he must go into the kingdom of heaven. This is inside the interconnectedness of his special woman. When the king finds the queen he is searching for, she will fill the void in his heart with overflowing love. She is the desire of his dreams, but he will never know who she is until their spirits are connected by unadulterated love.

Ladies, by now you know the kingdom is within you. Henceforth, I am convinced — along with the ancients — that the union between the man and woman brings God's power, love, and wisdom on earth and into our lives. Herein this gives us men all the resources necessary on earth to overcome life's challenges during our pursuit of success.

Having a woman with voluptuous curves is always a plus, but having a woman with a high level of consciousness, good cooking game, and wisdom is truly worth any king traveling the Seven Seas to search for her. This rings true, even if that means fighting lions, tigers, bears, or dragons along the way. These days, men fight to secure a queen by chasing checks in the 21st century against the rigors of unemployment and bills.

It is interesting enough that the Queen of Sheba (Queen Makeda) traveled to see King Solomon in Jerusalem. Queen Makeda was the queen of both Egypt and Ethiopia; long ago both African countries were vast empires feeding the entire world with scientific innovations, life-saving agriculture, and masonry. The queen came with great wealth to meet the king and to discuss big business in the maritime trade; not necessarily to hook up with him. Biblical scriptures teach us that Queen Sheba came with gifts to bless the king because of his wisdom, the organization of his business, wealth, and his physical appearance.[7] As a guest, it was custom to bring a gift back in those days, like it is today, despite if people were rich or poor; it's a way to bless their family and home.

Now the Bible, along with many other historical books, neglects to say much about Queen Makeda. Yet, it's been historically proven that she came from the land of Kush (Ethiopia, located in the eastern region of Africa). She was a great administrator, builder, and international stateswoman. Sometimes it's hard to separate legend from fact, but to give you an idea of her power, her empire included parts of Upper Egypt, Ethiopia, parts of Arabi, Syria, Armenia, India, and the whole region between the Mediterranean and the Erythraean Sea. A good mother will raise her daughter to be a woman of integrity and honor. Without a mother's guidance, a young lady can lose herself to the whirlwinds of the world.

Nevertheless, Queen Makeda's mother, Queen Ismenie, made it her business to prepare her daughter for her inevitable role as Queen of the Kushites (Ethiopia). In fact, before Egypt existed, it was part of the territory of the King of Kush (Nubia), King Menes. The women from Kush were some of the most prized women in the world for their wisdom, beauty, and, most importantly, their clairvoyance. Every man of regality wanted to marry a woman or have multiple wives from that region.

Ask yourself this question:

> "What are the women of my family,
> neighborhood, or city known for?"

(I hope it's something good!)

Are they known for keeping their home happy? Drama and bad attitudes? Prone for certain illnesses? Having a gentle heart, or staying in shape?

Ask yourself: what gifts do I bring to the table to catch the man of my dreams? There's heavy competition out there for a quality man, ladies. I want you to get beyond the cute smile, top-notch weave, and tight dresses. Show a good man that you are valuable and can take care of him and the home, prepare nutritious meals, manage money, support him in his business endeavors, raise your future kids with love, and stay committed to the team. Use your actions to show him that you're willing to go that extra mile, like the Queen of Sheba. You don't need a million dollars' worth of material gifts, but you will need the fruits of your gentle spirit to plant a million kisses on his heart — along with your priceless hugs and love. Use what you have to get to where you want to go. The fruits of your gentle spirit can kiss the heart.

A Woman's Intuition

The female has the capacity to measure the consciousness or quality of the male's Inner G, especially when he has enjoyed the fruits of her womb. The quality of a man's genuine love can be determined at this point. A woman's intuition is her greatest and strongest sense. If a man's spirit doesn't heal, inspire, or sustain you, then he is not the one. However, if he does, then you found the right man to crown. His spirit will charge your spirit and give you that positive electrical jolt of energy when you are down. His spirit will even uplift you higher when you are already elated and make love to your spirit around the clock. Once you reach this level of consciousness, physical intercourse will be a small treat in comparison to the rest of your journey. You two will have the potential to reach an ecstasy beyond anything you can think or imagine.

We control our own reality in the environment we share our energy. Positive people and places produce positive thoughts. Thoughts create positive outcomes. Positive outcomes produce a positive world. The same is true for negative thoughts.

A man loves a woman who can guide him to see the bigger picture: a brighter future with success at a magnanimous level. A woman of faith will see beyond what it looks like in the here and now. She lets her intuition guide her. She will uplift her man and those around her onto a cloud of consciousness to expand their expectations and engage their faith. Ladies, if you succeed in doing this in a genuine fashion, the gentleman of your dreams and reality will be one and the same. *Mr. Right* will fall head over heels for you. You are now the beholder of the secret to a gentleman's heart. Meet him at the place where he envisions himself in the future.

Ms. Marilyn Monroe

Most people don't know that Marilyn Monroe spent many years of her early life in an orphanage, and that her real name is Norma Jean Mortensen. During her time as an orphan, she learned how to entice boys — and later men — into doing what she desired them to do. Her diary noted that many males said she gave off vibrations that floored them by just saying a single word. She mastered the power of attraction as a teenager.

At the age of twenty-three, she spent hours in front of a mirror practicing her smile, flirtatious stares, and seductive walk before she would go out anywhere. She was the epitome of a sex siren and worked hard at maintaining that image because she knew it would bring her one thing: power. I am not insinuating that you should practice in front of the mirror, but I am telling you to invest more time in the image you project, including the way you look and smell.

Marilyn Monroe wasn't the first woman to master the art of seduction and influence men due to her beauty. Paris, a prince of Troy, started a war over Helen of Troy. Caesar took over the Egyptian empire for Cleopatra. General Napoleon faced embarrassment over his love for Joséphine de Beauharnais, and Arthur Miller experienced writer's block for years over a woman. These men were spellbound due to their love for women who held their hearts in their hands.

Sex Isn't Just Sex

Once your king enters your womb, he's crossing the threshold of your temple's portal and taking the course into your galaxy of stars. The potential to enter different dimensions of your world to get to know you on a deeper level is possible.

This is where we find new inspiration for our ideas. There is a sexual energy we all seek in our companions. In my opinion, a couple will find satisfaction difficult with their partner if their sexual energy doesn't match. Remember, sex isn't limited to a physical encounter; it's more powerful when it's a mental experience. When you have sex using your mind, instead of your genitals — you allow a higher consciousness of thinking. And, quite frankly, it's much safer than physical sex, which comes with the risk of catching STDs (sexually transmitted demons), unwanted pregnancies, and soul ties that we can't shake off.

The components that give a healthy couple the opportunity to have a real "orgasm" are mutual and mental harmony.[4] In today's society, we are conditioned to think we're having an orgasm when our physical bodies start to shake during sexual intercourse. We all know it takes energy to have a sexual encounter. However, if it's butt-naked, sweating-buckets-lovemaking until the sun rises, it takes tons of energy along mind-body connectedness.

Even when sperm travels into a woman's vagina, there must be a rhythm of the male's sperm to ejaculate in hopes of procreation; the heart must reach a certain level. The rhythm of the heart is the key for him to release his sperm. This is the impetus to life's cycle for humanity to keep progressing.

The rhythm of a woman's heart rate must also reach a certain level to have an orgasm. During this state, her eggs can receive the sperm needed to get pregnant, even though an orgasm isn't essential for the process. A real man will care about his queen reaching her climax, and he'll make it his business that you go first. A low-energy selfish companion will get his and go to sleep time after time.

The act of lovemaking should be used with purpose, according to the desires of the both of you. Sex should be liberating and about exploring the low and high levels of energy with the one you're in love with.

IRRESISTIBLE BEAUTY

Being a Sexy Queen has its perks. Many guys will whistle, gawk, admire, and approach you, and a few will have something intellectual to say. Attracting attention comes with the Sexy Queen territory, but it can distract you from noticing a genuine king who finds you irresistible. Being foxy is one thing, but being sexy with class is something else.

Dear Queen,

Your energy introduces you before you even speak a word. Wear your sexiness with confidence, but don't think for a second that your sexiness is your crown of glory. Your heart is the true crown, and your mind is the crown jewel. Your creativity alone will set you apart, making you the sexiest queen alive!

CHAPTER 9

SERVING QUEEN

A wife of noble character who can find?
She is worth far more than rubies.

- Proverbs 31:10

hen you are serving your king, you are serving God. The same goes when your man is serving you as his queen. The female and male relationship is a union of God that represents the balance of the spirit, mind, and body. It is important for women to understand this concept, as you are the creators of the home where balance is perfected. The art of serving doesn't stop with your mate, but it is also important to serve your community.

In the book of Genesis, the Bible talks about how Abraham sent his most trusted servant to find a good wife for his son. Abraham's wife, Sarah, had passed away, and he gave specific instructions to prohibit his son from marrying any Canaanite women. The family's bloodline was at stake. Perhaps the ways of the Canaanite women disgusted him, such as what or whom they worshipped or how they carried themselves or treated their guests. Abraham revered his deceased wife and wanted a woman as virtuous as her for his prized son Isaac. The lineage was on the line.

If only parents of today would give this more thought when they give away their child's hand in marriage. Allowing the wrong person (spirit) into the family could sabotage the family's legacy. Most parents with a kingdom mindset will take extra measures to ensure the longevity of the family's assets and work rigorously to match their child with a wealthy consort.

Sarah was a woman of great faith and a Proverbs 31 woman — a very rare breed. This type of woman is honored by the community. Her children and husband sing her praises. She makes profitable business deals for herself and on her husband's behalf, and she can pick out land to cultivate it for crops. She helps the poor and prepares meals for her family in the mornings and evenings. Her mouth is filled with wisdom and not curses. Old-school folks will tell you that women of this caliber are becoming extinct. God knows I hope this isn't true.

A woman with a heart to serve is powerful. One of the most unattractive attributes in a female is conceit and the unwillingness to serve her guests and her community. Refusing to cater to those under your care shows you don't have what it takes to be a leader. A great leader understands how to treat everyone as royalty. Someone who has served others understands the balance of power and shows empathy toward other servants.

A king will want a woman who can cater to him, his children, and his guests. An average man may not care about his woman being a great hostess, but it matters to a well-off man. Every man wants to feel like a king beside his queen. I'm not talking about bowing down, washing his feet with your hair, or compromising your core values to please his ego. What I'm referring to is exhibiting class, letting go of any degenerate family traditions, and creating your own traditions together.

One of the greatest compliments a man can receive from his friends and family about his woman is her excellence in hospitality. I guess you can say it's a pride thing. A good woman who can cook and serve her man with love makes men feel powerful!

There's nothing wrong with a man being proud to have you as his queen, and vice versa. In fact, that is a sign of an excellent relationship. You want to have a man who feels like he can rule the world with you by his side. Now, I know some women will read this and say, "I don't have time for all that." I suggest you start making time, because families are being torn apart. The greatest relationships are those that serve and uplift each other.

My mother was raised in Haiti and spent the latter part of her life in Florida. She loved to serve cold drinks in fancy glasses on top of a saucer to her children and all her guests: young or old, male or female — it didn't matter. I felt special when she brought me an ice-cold beverage in the living room. Now that I'm a grown man, I can't remember anyone serving me or anyone else a drink on a saucer. When people were in my mother's home, she wanted them to know they were in a house of class. This was Haitian hospitality at its finest.

When a woman consistently shows her ability to lovingly serve her king, then that man knows she has the potential of being a great mother (if he is wise). Her children will stand to bless her, and her husband will praise her. Men are visual creatures, so you will have to show us that you are a Proverbs 31:10, Michelle Obama type of woman. It's a bad look when a woman is selfish and too conceited to take care of anyone but herself; this limits her growth and development. It's a huge turn-off when one does something for others only when one gets something in return.

THE ANGELS OF PEARL HARBOR

On December 7, 1941, the nurses at the U.S. Naval Hospital at Pearl Harbor earned their medals. They were blitzed with more than

3,000 wounded soldiers, pedestrians, and children. Twenty American ships were destroyed or damaged along with 300 airplanes. As you could imagine, it was straight pandemonium.

The Hawaiian Naval base never knew what hit them and, to make matters worse, most of the casualties occurred on the naval battleship U.S.S. Arizona. The Japanese hit the naval base with a surprise air attack that shell-shocked everyone. There were 524 nurses, along with 114 registered nurses from the Red Cross to help with the emergency. Morphine, first aid kits, and other supplies were running out fast, so nurses had to make split-second decisions regarding the patients and their conditions.

When the markers ran out, the resourceful nurses used their lipsticks to mark the wounded with "M" for morphine, "C" for critical care, and "F" for fatally wounded. Blood, bullets, fires, and screaming surrounded them.[1]

They had to decide who to save and who to let die a slow death. You had to be a brave person with a tough stomach in order to operate in such a chaotic scene. The situation was so bad that convalescent patients who'd asked to return to duty were granted permission to do the best they could to help. It was a gruesome, hell-on-earth scene; however, these women held their own. I tip my crown to these heroines!

These nurses served their country with honor and bravery. To get a better picture of the situation, watch the movie *Pearl Harbor* starring Kate Beckinsale and Ben Affleck. It's a terrific film with a fabulous love story. I grew fond of all nurses after watching this movie and reading about the war. The nurses proved their resourcefulness, determination, and valor. They received an impressive 1,619 medals and commendations during the war and were awarded Silver Stars for their extraordinary courage under fire. More than 200 Army nurses lost their lives while serving others during the attack. Sixteen medals were awarded posthumously to nurses who died because of enemy fire.

The aftermath of the Pearl Harbor attacks created opportunities to empower women. When they returned home to the states, the Army nurses were given the ability to seek additional education under the G.I. Bill of Rights, which allowed them to pursue professional educational goals. Their stellar performance during the war raised the self-esteem of nurses around the world, as well as the confidence in American women. Society's perception of nursing shifted to a valued profession. Their performance under the most strenuous circumstance planted the seeds for the creation of the Women's Army Auxiliary Corps (WAAC), which became law in May 1942. It opened the door for women to join the military. The former First Lady, Eleanor Roosevelt, pushed the envelope to get the Women's Naval Reserve and the Marine Corps Women's Reserve.

Those women were one-of-a-kind. When a man is going to war, he hopes the woman in his life will stand up to the plate. He will know through trial and error that you're already there without having to ask. Having trust in your spouse allows you to direct your energy into more important areas.

SERVING ISN'T SLAVERY

There isn't a real man who wants a non-submissive wife, despite her fineness or wealth. Being able to submit makes you even sexier; however, it's your heart that has to submit. It's one thing to serve your king grudgingly, but the beauty comes from serving him, your family, and community because your heart is in it. It allows your king to submit to you as well. And when I say submit, I'm talking about submitting through love and not fear. Ladies, when a mature man says he wants a woman who is submissive, don't freak out. He is trying to articulate that he wants a woman who is cooperative, respectful, and willing to understand him. That's all.

There are far too many women running around bucking and kicking their way through life while having to answer to no one. Any sense of discipline from a male counterpart scares them away from a lasting relationship. At the first sign of trouble, they're out the door. I guarantee that he will protect and provide for you even more once you've consented to his authority. Your actions or non-actions will speak volumes. Who has time to enervate their energy by bickering over who wears the pants in the relationship? Who cares?! This will cause you to operate on a low level of consciousness, constantly at each other's throats instead of uplifting each other's spirit, hence activating petty behaviors and violence/abuse in relationships.

GEISHA

Every culture has a tradition of servitude. In Japan, the teenage odoriko "dancing girls" were paid to serve their guests by dancing elegantly for them. In the 1680s, the purpose of the odoriko was to give pleasure to the upper-class samurai warriors. The odoriko paved the way for what we now know as the geisha — a Japanese hostess trained to entertain men with conversation, dance, and song. A one-stop-shop.

An entire culture was built around men seeking women whose sole purpose was to serve them. The role of a geisha was an honored position, and the servitude of a woman was very important and sacred to the Japanese culture. In fact, they created the "Way of Tea," which we call the Japanese Tea Ceremony. This tradition was intended to demonstrate their respect through grace and superb etiquette.

PRINCESS DIANA

"I'd like to be a queen in people's hearts but I don't see myself being queen of this country." – Princess Diana

Diana Frances, the Princess of Wales, was born on July 1, 1961 and passed away on August 30, 1997. Many of us are familiar that she died with the press chasing her, but let me share how the Princess lived once she discovered who she truly was — a serving angel at heart. Princess Diana lived the last years of her life in the public's view as the wife of Prince Charles of Wales, the son of Queen Elizabeth II.

Through marriage into the royal family, Princess Diana amassed a significant amount of wealth. She may have worn fancy clothes, but her life was the exact opposite. Prince Charles' extramarital affair(s) were eating her alive, but there is always a silver lining at the end of a dark cloud. The strenuous relationship with her husband made her want to find her true self. She redeemed herself through her contributions as a humanitarian and philanthropist. In a recorded video interview, she stated the following powerful words:

> "I was always very ambitious. There was a
> profound sense of destiny for my life!"[2]

She was obviously courageous, leaving behind her shiny glass image and walking away from the royal dungeon that her loveless marriage created. Princess Diana realized that her husband was not looking for love — he wanted someone to share the burdens of the kingdom. Love was not on Charles' heart or mind. In fact, he confirmed it during their first interview as a couple when he said,

"I think I'm in love."

Red flags should have gone up for the princess, but they were already married at that point. His statement set the tone that there wasn't going to be a "love flight" between them. It was inevitable that the marriage was doomed from the beginning. Once she walked away from the crown, she began to embrace her true self and purpose as a woman of power in a world filled with hopeless children waiting for her. This proves that money isn't everything.

She was undoubtedly one of the most admired, influential, and best-loved women of our time. She took trips around the world to give impoverished children hope, love, food, and hugs. Princess Diana found her inner power and personal fulfillment when she became involved with various charities, including The British Red Cross. She managed to put her personal dilemma (marriage failure) aside when it came to helping people. She could have easily given up on herself and her life's purpose, but she chose to transform the negative energy around her into making a positive difference. A true mark of a queen!

She should've dethroned Queen Elizabeth II and taken over Britain. Her relationship with Prince Charles was toxic to her energy, and it was evident that she was in a "royal cage." She began to live freely once she moved out of the palace and became the queen she always desired. Princess Diana was praised as one of Britain's most fashionable women, but she was globally known for her philanthropy. Lady Di didn't need a public relations campaign — she was naturally a bright light. A true gem! Her actions showed that she was all heart and compassion for others, which is the most important attribute anyone can bring to the table.

Princess Diana didn't wait until she had money and power to help others. She started working with children at the age of nineteen and became a teacher's assistant at Young England Nursery. She came back to her natural roots in an even bigger way toward the last years of her life. Once she found her purpose, she continued raising her two boys, Prince William and Prince Harry, and dove whole-heartedly into a tremendous amount of charity work. It was said that Princess Diana knew every detail of the charities she supported, and she impressed people by remembering their names. It was not a regular royal visit with flowers, red carpet, and regal waves. She was different — her approach and care were genuine. She never did anything to look good for the cameras.

Princess Diana truly had a "Queen's Heart!" She accomplished extraordinary things with her power. Lady Di supported more than one hundred charities (both physically and financially), including the International Campaign to Ban Landmines, which won the Nobel Peace Prize. When the picture of the princess holding an amputee child from Angola surfaced, it gave her charity work international exposure. A picture is worth a thousand words, but Princess Diana's photo with the children was worth a thousand news articles!

She knew the press would take hundreds of pictures of her, so she used her star power to grab the landmine victim and refused to take any pictures without the child on her lap — very admirable of her. As if that wasn't enough, Princess Diana walked through a landmine field and ensuring that the press took plenty of pictures. She understood the power of public relations. During her time in Angola, she told a reporter:

"I'm not a political figure, nor do I want to be one. But I come with my heart, and I want to bring awareness to people in distress, whether it's in Angola or any part of the world. The fact is I'm a humanitarian figure. Always have been and always will be."[2]

Within three days, world leaders changed the laws on landmines, which were responsible for killing and maiming 15,000 to

20,000 people a year. She worked fifteen-hour schedules for two days, while visiting landmine victims of Bosnia. Most of her visits were purposely private without cameras or press allowed. Her landmine campaign was her greatest triumph without a doubt. Her dream came true a few months after she passed away. The last year of her life was also the best year of her life. The profound image with the African child and the princess helped influence the signing of the Mine Ban Treaty in December 1997 to end the use of anti-personnel landmines.

Many people of power spend more hours tending to their business outside of their home than with their family because they are so concerned with their public image. Princess Di wasn't one of those women. She left her two princes close to thirty million dollars and gave detailed instructions to her mother for their education in the event that she went to heaven. Due to her generosity, she also left $80,000 (tax-free) to her butler Paul Burrell.

If there is anything that a king desires, it is a thoughtful, kind, fun, and genuine woman. Princess Diana was all of that and then some! Princess Diana was, without a doubt, what my apostle Yvette Brinson calls "a distribution center!" She distributed her wealth and love to those in need of it. By no stretch of the imagination was she a fantasy. As proof to her loving legacy, her work continues today through the Diana, Princess of Wales Memorial Fund.

Lady Diana may have graced hundreds of magazine covers, including *People* magazine more than fifty times and *Time* magazine seven times, but I truly believe she would've given up her fame and fortune to save more children. She walked away from the fairy tale façade lifestyle and embraced her true self. She was such a blessed woman, and her actions created blessings that forever changed families, communities, and even nations and generations to come.

Becoming a Proverbs 31:10 woman may not be one of your goals, and maybe it's never crossed your mind until now. A Serving Queen is in high demand in every aspect of society: home, schools, churches, and the corporate world. We may not hear heroine stories of the likes of Princess Diana or the Pearl Harbor nurses, but the ability to help those in need lies in every woman.

Dear Queen,

*There are many ways to serve others,
whether it's your community, family, or
king. Serving isn't slavery – it's an honor.*

CHAPTER 10

WISE QUEEN

*I*n the classic relationship book *Men Are from Mars, Women Are from Venus*, Dr. Robert Gray cleverly created a score chart for women to use.

I've used a mental score card ever since I can remember to give and take away points from a young lady I dated. She'll get "cool points" if she loves to wear dresses, shows kindness, avoids selfishness, loves to cook, and wears her natural hair. Dr. Gray broke it down to help women understand vulnerable situations, such as becoming more supportive and less condescending toward their man. In other words, instead of upper-cutting their man when he makes a mistake, use wisdom to look at the silver lining and help him understand how he screwed up.

Here are some examples of the score card:

Number four: He gets lost, but she sees the good in the situation and says, "We would never have seen this beautiful sunset if we had taken the most direct route." (20-30 points)

Number fifteen: When he asks her to do something, she says yes and stays in a good mood (10 points).

My two favorites are numbers seventeen and eighteen: She is happy to see him when he gets home and greets him with a warm embrace (20 points); and she starts appreciating him again when he does little things for her to make up after a fight (30 points).

LOVE POINTS

When a man loses his job, or means of income, he is in a vulnerable state and will be angry with himself. He will need you to shine your love on him more than ever. The last thing he wants to feel is that he can't provide, protect, and support you. You'll be surprised how many times I've seen women use this opportunity to tear their man down. A man's whole psyche will change. He may not even be able to get it up during this time. If he is a real man, he'll pull through. You can't keep a good man down. If he's down on his luck, then he may seek refuge in lower level behaviors, such as drinking or smoking in excess or domestic violence to prove his manliness since he cannot be the breadwinner.

Your man can become a human hurricane on his way to self-destruct or die down, so get out of the way and don't try to fix it. A man must be willing to find his own way out of his quicksand or he'll end up back in it. You can lose the relationship, or worse, lose yourself trying to find him. A man must fight his own battles. He'll need you in the overall war. His happiness is not your responsibility. His happiness, just like your own, is solely his duty, not yours.

This is the perfect time to direct your love energy toward uplifting him. In doing so, you'll remind him that you two are in this together — through thick and thin. It is wise to assist him from a distance. You will get one million points! In fact, you will win his heart all over again. Relationships are exhausting until we teach each other how to direct our efforts in ways our partner can fully appreciate.

Queen Jezebel

The power of your words can build up or destroy a person's spirit. Words from another man don't bother or inspire fellas like the words of a woman. For instance, Queen Jezebel, Phoenician royalty in the ninth century B.C., was a perfect example of how to destroy a man and why that should never be the aim of any woman. She's mentioned heavily in biblical text and other history books.

Jezebel completely turned King Ahab's heart cold. She turned her king away from worshiping Yahweh (God) and persuaded him to worship other gods (Baal and Asherah). Jezebel was a licentious woman who knew her powers. She also influenced the saints of God to worship her gods. Legend has it that she met her demise after being thrown out of a window and ravaged by wild dogs.

Some of the negative attitudes being promoted on television and social media are ratchet: the terms "Boss B---h" and "Queen B---h" are nothing more than the Jezebel spirit coming back to life. Power in the wrong hands speaks volumes and can go wrong real quick. Queen Jezebel spit her venom whenever she could at her subjects. Most people have this misconception that all queens are good, but clearly that isn't true.

Be Mindful

A sensible man knows that a happy wife means a happy life, so he will not have a problem with you running the home. Keeping the peace is the name of the game. Also, he'll gladly oblige his queen's "honey-do list" requests. He will never want you to be without what makes you happy if it's realistically attainable within his power. Open his heart and he'll give you the world. It's only the insecure nature of a caveman who becomes offended and prohibits you from standing on the throne beside him. If you see these signs in your gentlemen, then you should run away — immediately. Keep in mind that the whole point of being together is to merge your kingdoms so that you can establish dominion.

Ladies, internalize whatever feelings a man has about himself. The hatred some men have for themselves will seep into your spirit through shared energy, whether it's through sex, conversations, or just hanging out. You are co-creating with a man of hate, a soldier in Satan's army, or possibly the devil himself. He doesn't appreciate the greatness in you, but he simply wants to take your powerful image to destroy you.

Some men want to drag down a sister who's doing well for herself; breaking you to the lowest level possible (his reptilian nature), so he can suck all your passion dry. He's not in love with the goddess in you. To this caveman, you are only good for a nut and to be butt-naked, barefoot, and cooking. A rational woman knows not to live by her emotions, especially if those emotions come in waves, in which he can easily recognize and then proceed to manipulate you.

Types of Women Who Push Good Men Away:

1) Drama Queens

2) Naggers

3) Lazy

4) Negative

5) Rude

6) Non-cooking

7) Unintelligent

Red Flags You're with the Wrong Man:

• Always talks about sex

- Never seeks to please you

- Never congratulates you on your successes

- Never has anything positive to say about you and/or women

- Non-supportive of your projects/career

- Conversations are rarely about future plans with you

- Won't pray with you

Check List of a Good Man:

1. Consistent in positive energy

2. Man of his word

3. Listens to you attentively

4. Hardworking

5. Never quits!

6. Supports your dreams

7. Protective of you and your home

THE SEVEN CHAKRAS

The lowest level of the seven Chakras is the Root Chakra located in the base of your spine. The Chakra system comes from Kemet (ancient Egypt) thousands of years ago. They believed that a person could achieve "God consciousness" if, and only if, one is willing and able to master their physical body and uplift his/her spiritual being. Spirituality is a personal relationship with the divine. The Chakra system's purpose was to measure your level of consciousness. The queens and Pharaohs of Kemet were considered godlike because they were reflections of what God would do if the Creator manifested in the physical form.

Love is the first level of higher consciousness that one can obtain after mastering the lower-level Chakras. Love is the fourth Chakra out of the seven. The Crown Chakra is the seventh, and highest, Chakra. In the pursuit of enlightenment, a woman must be able to love righteously and have compassion. As tough as the world is today, a man yearns to come home to the gentle and nurturing touch of his woman, his queen. He does not want to come home to a castle that has turned into a dungeon due to the continual cold shoulders you give him. It is better to live alone than to live in an unhappy home. The two of you must put your egos aside and come to a meeting of the minds so that you can "win."

Chakras are energy centers in the body. Your consciousness is a powerful weapon or curse, depending on which level you're on. Chakras are a way of measuring one's conscious state of enlightenment, as well as the recognition of one's self. Look at Chakras in the form of a ladder. The higher up you go, the clearer your mind becomes. The lower your position on the ladder, the more work you must do to develop the connection between the spirit and matter, mind and body. A man mentally stuck on the lower part of the ladder will only think and dwell upon survival.

Thoughts of Affirmation

Thoughts are powerful. Our ancestors from the Nile River civilizations went through thousands upon thousands of years of studying, researching, and testing the power of the mind and heart. They somehow figured out that the power of thought was just as powerful as words. Both can create a physical reality if we focus on them hard enough. Therefore, love creates life and anger creates destruction. The former is focused on uplifting and intimacy, while the latter brings you down. The happier you are, the more efficient your heart's electrical system will pump blood throughout your body.

"Death and life are in the power of the tongue, and those who love it will eat its fruits." Proverbs 18:21

Words spoken in righteous love will be received as a gift of gold to your soul. It feels wonderful when the opposite sex compliments your fashion style, smile, or accomplishments. A transfer of positive energy just took place from a god to a goddess. It makes us smile and glow throughout the day. Think of words as presents, and give them as often as possible. That positive energy bounces right back to you.

RIDE THE WAVES

Energy comes in two forms: cycles and waves. You can ride the waves of love, also known as ecstasy, once you become cognizant of them. There isn't a sex position in the world that will help you reach ecstasy, because it's based on a powerful connection between two people. Making true love, or "worship sessions," will become powerful; you will reach other dimensions. You must trust in yourself and your companion to catch the energy wave of your partner.

A man who finds a good wife finds treasure, because enlightenment begins at this point. A woman's intimacy with a man can get closer than anyone can. The divine connection of both the female and male energy has an opportunity to combine forces. Healthy partnerships are the key to a successful life. There is no way one person, male or female, can view everything from all angles. That's the beauty of having two pairs of eyes. The wisdom of a good woman is of immeasurable value to a man with a vision. Now he can win in areas of life that he was losing before, and your king will make you strong in your weak areas. Your love energy brings balance and order into his life, and his love energy will reciprocate that balance into your life if it's righteous.

Our brains are supercomputers with two hemispheres: the right and the left. The right side is the spiritual side (fantasy, spirituality, faith, future, etc.), and the left holds the physical aspects (reality, rationality, language, details, etc.). We can only use one side in full capacity at a time. When we have a meeting of the minds, it allows our two halves to become one, which turns our brains into mega computers. Maintaining a positive mindset helps it to work at optimal levels. What we feed into our mind is the fuel it uses to operate.

Steps to Create Positive Energy:

- Pray and meditate more.

- Sing, laugh, and dance.

- Write and recite poetry.

- Eat more fruits and vegetables.

- Conduct a relationship detox.

- Go jogging.

- Read uplifting spiritual books.

- Watch comedy movies.

We've all heard of the phrase "tying the knot." It's a cliché for people who just got married. I asked myself: where do these clichés come from? After conducting internet research, studying the Bible and old books on ancient civilizations, I discovered that our ancestors believed tying the knot was the union of an independent woman and creating a home and family life. They believed it was the beginning of true wisdom symbolized by joining the woman, hence the term soul tie — tying the knot, the combining of two worlds and two souls.

The idea of wisdom begins with the mother. The mother is every child's first teacher and nurturer. Naturally, it's the mother's responsibility to care for newborn babies from birth. She is the only one who can breastfeed the child. A baby's first lessons are from the mother. Therefore, a child's foundation of wisdom comes from her as well.

Mothers are, in fact, the creator of a child. Ancient African women were the first to build houses, villages, agricultural sciences, schools, produce marketplaces, and establish laws and systems of governance. Having created all of this, she became the throne of power from which men were to rule. This is where the "Black Woman is God" belief developed.

Because the knot has no beginning and end, it is therefore eternal, hence the creation of the term "eternal knot." It is also known as the wisdom knot. In Ghana, the people of Akan highly revered the "wisdom knot" as a symbol of wisdom, ingenuity, intelligence, and patience. It conveys the idea that a wise person can choose the best possible means to attain a goal. Two people who bring their wisdom together have tied the knot to live together for eternity. Because their spirits and bodies are so intertwined, their jubilation has no beginning or end.

It's the parents' hope that their child will grow beautiful and strong to one day marry someone who will continue the family's lineage. The knot continues to symbolize the combination of knowledge and wisdom in a unified focus. In the case of a family, home, and marriage, it perpetuates a new life in the world. The ability to think jointly and combine energy forces to work together for one objective removes selfish thinking and eliminates focusing only on oneself to bring an idea into fruition.

"...If you prize wisdom, she will make you great. Embrace her, and she will honor you. She will place a lovely wreath (crown) on your head; she will present you with a beautiful crown" (Proverbs 4:5-9).

WISDOM KNOT AND COMFORT

In a forthcoming work, *7 Types of Kings, Queens Desire*, I explain why men fight to the death to protect their woman's honor. One thing is for certain: our ancestors from a long time ago comprehended that a man's source of power and strength came from his queen.

The connection was so deep between women and men, feminine and masculine energies, that the pharaohs of Kemet buried themselves with images of Nuit, the Sky Goddess, painted and/or engraved on the inside of the lid of their lavish coffins. This illustration enabled the feminine principle to remain with the pharaohs for all of eternity.

The comfort of a woman's breast on her man's chest is one of the most intimate moments for a couple. Our wise ancestors wanted that comfort for eternity, so why can't men experience this heaven on earth now? There is no reason we can't if we believe women are the most sacred entity in the world. Not only because of the joy from the physical interchange with her, but especially due to the enlightenment and growth that can be garnered from those intimate encounters.

DEGREES OF WISDOM

Once upon a time, people could not get married until they demonstrated certain degrees of wisdom, as well as acquired skills to take care of themselves and their spouse. In this case, they would become a blessing instead of a burden to themselves and, more importantly, to their community. One had to go through a rite of passage to show themselves approved. This principle should be reapplied today because we live in a fast-paced world that doesn't prepare people for marriage and life. How in the world can one get married if they can't tend to their own needs and responsibilities? This is the number one reason divorces have skyrocketed since the 1970s. Many couples should not have tied the knot in the first place. The demonstration of wisdom was never questioned and did not exist. There are no rites of passage for marriage in America. We throw ourselves lavish parties and tie the knot. Boom, we're married now!

From all my research over the years, it appears that the Primal Mother was the creator and founder of institutionalized education.

Therein, she was associated with the attribute of wisdom. Taking heed to wisdom will save a man's life, money, and dreams. Men are prone to make a lot of silly mistakes, especially when we don't have our "better half." Exhibit that you are a well of wisdom and a jackpot to be with! You will have no issue from your king asking to take your hand in marriage. Wisdom and intelligence are a huge turn-on for both sexes.

Combining two worlds, two psyches, and two energy forces isn't the easiest thing in the world to do. In fact, it must be one of the most difficult aspects of life, especially in the twenty-first century with all the distractions (e.g., smartphones, iPods, iPads, Internet, social media, newspapers, news stations, television, magazines, wars, recessions, etc.), including sexual messages constantly pushed through the media. Despite all the aforementioned, we are still able to find love if we keep wisdom close. We are told that love conquers all, but in reality, it's our wise actions with love that conquer all. Where there is hope, there is love and wisdom.

Dear Queen,

*The power of your words can be used
to build up or to destroy a man. Words
from another man don't bother or inspire
fellas like the words of a woman.*

CHAPTER 11

ENERGY OF
BOTH WORLDS

*M*en and women give and receive energy in waves and cycles differently. Energy cannot be destroyed or created; however, the flow of it can be magnified or decreased in our lives. Energy is indestructible. Everything becomes simple to understand when it's broken down to energy. Understanding what type of energy your partner is bringing into your world makes a difference.

"You took the words right out of my mouth!"

Have you ever spoken with a friend or family member who said something you were just about to say?

This happens when you are around people who are operating on the same wavelength or are in tune with your vibrational frequency. It's a beautiful experience when you don't have to fully explain everything because you're building an empire with someone who completely understands you — they get it! This may take months, years, or even decades, but it must happen to build up your relationship's

189

"keeping power." Without this vibrational frequency, your relationship will be limited and strenuous.

On the contrary, when we are around people who don't understand us and are on a different level of vibrations (positive or negative), it causes friction, confusion, and, periodically, physical altercations. There are tons of people in relationships who could avoid friction and wasted energy if they removed themselves from these predicaments. Time is energy, and we must use it wisely. A woman should be an inspirational and motivating force, directing her energy to uplift her man. If he refuses to understand you, then you should separate yourself from his equation and life. The angelic essence of a woman's self-image and confidence is distorted when they are tainted with men who do not appreciate their graciousness.

Queens, please don't sell yourselves short. Sell your talents. Go for a man who wants to appreciate you rather than one who wants you because he finds you sexy. Being attractive does count, so don't get it twisted. Men need much more than a beauty queen or a trophy wife. These women look good, but only a small percentage of them are humble.

The energy we all truly want (whether we admit it or not) is to find someone who increases our love energy. Everything is energy — our kisses, hugs, home-cooked meals, lovemaking, business deals, text messaging, talking, running, sleeping, breathing, and so on. What kind of energy do you want to build with your king? Every woman has the key to a certain man's destiny.

We are opposite on many levels, but are we trying to become one and the same? When a female is in her feelings stage, the male is trying to analyze the cause of her negative emotions, which is the thinking stage. Ladies, you don't want your man to always stay in the thinking stage. We aren't built that way. Most of us just want to relax and enjoy the pleasures of your presence.

Spiritual Energy

Energy makes the world go round. We can't breathe without the energy to inhale and exhale. Our level of energy predicts our next move and distant future. Energy is as precious as time itself. It's what we do with our energy within a given time and space that determines our spirit. One can never separate from his or her energy and spirit.

In the ancient culture of Kemet, a person who follows Maat principles was called a god or goddess. Maat, pronounced Mah-aught, was the ancient Egyptian spiritual concept of truth, balance, order, law, justice, and morality. Practicing this spiritual belief enabled the people to keep their energy electric and focused. Maat was a way of life, and it kept individual relationships and the populace in check without the enforcement of a government.

Power of Sexual Energy

A man does not want a woman with a sex addiction, and if you truly have a sex addiction, then it's recommended you seek professional help. Excessive sex and sex addictions weaken the physical body as well as the mind. Birth control pills and contraceptives all add to the hypersexuality and massive reproductive failures, impotency, venereal diseases, and poor-quality sperm and eggs.[1] Sex was never meant to be just a casual event. Sexual energy is far too powerful to play games with.

Strength of Your Divine Words

Reassure that you have your man's best intentions in mind by backing up your divine words with actions. The love in our relationships will continue to evaporate until we learn how to direct our energies in ways that our partner can fully appreciate. This allows their love reflection to reciprocate in the relationship, while keeping the love flight in the air. Learn to go with the flow in the *right* path. A man will need your divine energy to continue in the right direction. Keep the following in mind to push your king forward:

1. As he begins to step out to reach his dream, remind him that all help and provision will come to him from the universe.

2. Going against the grain is expected.

3. Don't let popular opinions cause him to lose sight of what God has shown him.

When he wins, you win. That is why you should do your best to support him.

Words have life and potency with a life span determined by our usage. New words are created often in dictionaries, replacing the old words we cease to speak through our pens. The power of divine words that we speak through our spirit can place people under hypnosis. Using words to influence or control people is an art form that has made many people rich and famous for centuries. Hindus and Greeks have used this ancient art form in the sleep temples to help cure people since the fifth century B.C.[2]

The brain is an epicenter that operates as a success or failure mechanism. The data we feed it will determine what our life's journey and environment will produce. If one can control his or her anger, meditate, and master the functions of the brain, then one's body and physical reality will conform to what the brain commands. Our brain is a supercomputer with ten to twenty billion brain cells and neurons. It fires electricity in the form of neurotransmitters. Think of each brain cell as a gigabyte of memory for a computer. Each brain cell is capable of recalling, transmitting, receiving, and recording knowledge. The brain is truly a terrible thing to waste, and so are our words.

> "The tongue has the power of life and
> death, and those who love it will eat
> its fruit." (Proverbs 18:21 NIV)

As a goddess, you will resurrect your man's spirit with your divine words, and your words will be well received.

Kemetan priests were also scientists that practiced maithuna — the total mental, spiritual, and physical engagement between a woman and man. They believed that a man had to connect to the divine feminine energy of a loving woman to truly know God. If priests weren't hooked up with the female energy by their own free will, then the men were limited in their knowledge from the Creator. The woman's energy opens his mind so that he can receive a celestial message from God. They were conscious of the sacredness of love-making to tap into the powers of divinity within them.

For sexual energy of jubilation to take place, the meeting of the minds must occur prior to joining physical bodies with your king. Then, you can meet in spirit because you waited to see if there was enough energy for a spiritual connection to materialize. Merging two worlds is a spiritual act, and by skipping this step, you've set a timer for an implosion. It's only a matter of time before the relationship takes a plunge.

Allow your words to be the air beneath the wings of your love plane.

QUEEN QUIZ: WHAT TYPE OF QUEEN ARE YOU?

1. What are the top two complaints you've received in your current or past relationships?

   _____

2. What are the top two things men in your current or past relationships praised you for?

   _____

3. With what you've just read thus far, how are you going to improve yourself starting today?

   _____

MAKING AN ELECTRIC CONNECTION

If you place your hands on someone who has a key in an electrical socket, you will instantly get shocked too. That's how life works when we are connected to people. The aura of an individual has the power to either keep your vibrations up, down, or on a rollercoaster ride with many highs and lows. When your heart is connected to a man with a lot of energy, you will be pumped up as well. Those electrical currents will run through the both of you.

In *The Last Samurai*, starring the beautiful Japanese actress Koyuki Kato and Tom Cruise, Koyuki helps Cruise with his Yoroi (Samurai armor suit). She takes her time, dressing him gracefully. Koyuki placed her hands over his body without ever touching him, as if to energize him with her love energy and strength. An unseen

194

energy left her hands and poured into his spirit. Their eyes kissed, and in that moment, you realize they have fallen in love with each other. This scene blew my mind! They made love without taking off their clothes; love from love is a spiritual matter we all deserve.

That is why women should avoid people, especially men, who have a negative or unwanted attraction toward them. His hate spirit will try to have intercourse with your spirit. Even though he may not be successful in doing so physically, he will plant toxic seeds in your brain, and may eventually become triumphant with a significant amount of time and seductive gestures. The flesh and the brain become weaker when you stop soaking up knowledge.

You should strengthen your body (exercise), mind (read), and spirit (pray/meditate) on a regular basis. And some of you may have to do this more than others, according to your life's position. When you acknowledge the Holy Spirit, and embrace your Divine spirit inside, God is able to work.

The world will come at you one hundred thousand ways to distract you from praying, meditating, and seeking peace. That is why you must make your spiritual connection directly with God a priority. This fellowship is vitally important for one simple reason: God is limitless. Through prayer, we can find light and strength amid our darkest hour to push forward. Light is symbolic of knowledge, wisdom, and understanding.

Dear Queen,

God will guide our spirits with strength,
perseverance, endurance, and (my favorite),
COURAGE! A vivacious woman who
isn't afraid to pray on the spot is probably
the most powerful person on earth. You
hold the keys to the gateway of heaven
and victory in the battles of life.

CHAPTER 12

WARRIOR QUEEN

*I*t brings me great pleasure to introduce several fearless queens you must get to know. Fear is an illusion, and a warrior queen will make sure her king remembers that during times of battle. We create fear when we use our energy to focus on the end result we hope to avoid. There are battles in life that we must win — come hell or high water.

The Ashanti women tapped on the ground with clubs and spears and warned their men that they would be maimed and killed should they retreat from the battleground in fear. This pushed the male Ashanti warriors to think hard. Thus, they would return home without a victory.

This may have been why the Ashanti of West Africa were one of the last indigenous nations to fall in the face of European colonial expansion. Queen Yaa Asantewa, Great Queen of Courage, gave a motivational speech to her people that if the men did not go and fight off the invaders, then she would organize all the women to fight in their place.[1] Talk about a call to action! Your man will entertain fear if you allow the culture of timidity to develop within your home and your kingdom.

You must become a one-woman army when needed for your family's protection, especially your children. Your bravery will turn a real man on; he will know that he isn't the only warrior. There is no need for either of you to fight all your battles alone. Life is more fun when a god and goddess take on the world together. It takes two!

Would Barack Obama have been president without Mrs. Obama by his side? Would Theodore Roosevelt have integrated the United States Air Force without the aid of Eleanor Roosevelt? Would the nation of Angola have been able to fight off the Portuguese for more than 30 years from enslavement without the leadership of Queen Nzinga? We don't know. But one thing we do know for sure is that these powerful women played significant roles in the success of their countries.

Dr. Cheikh Anta Diop, a Senegalese writer, physicist, and anthropologist, once stated, "Many African women were great militarists and on occasion led their armies in battle (Harriet Tubman did the same in 1863 for the Union Army). Long before they knew of the existence of Europe, the Africans had produced a way of life where men were secure enough to let women advance as far as their talent would take them."[1]

QUEEN NZINGA

Queen Nzinga, Ana de Sousa Nzinga Mbande (1583-1663), was born to King Kiluanji and Queen Kangela, who ruled the Kingdoms of Matamba and Ndongo (Modern day Congo). Nzinga almost died in her mother's womb after the umbilical cord wrapped around her neck. According to tradition, this was a sign that the person would be proud and tough. And she was both, indeed!

Even though Nzinga had a brother, Mbandi, and two sisters, Kifunji and Mukambu, she was, without a doubt, her father's favorite. Her prowess in hunting was music to her father's ears. She gained favor from her father by spending quality time with him during hunting expeditions, where training for warriors took place. Princess Nzinga had more guts and warrior skills than brother, who was next in line to be king.

I'm not saying that you need to be a Queen Nzinga, the Afrikan leader who defied and defeated the Portuguese from invading her country for 30 years. On the contrary, you'll have to show a man that you're ready and able to go to war to protect your family and his dreams. Show him you are willing to put it all on the line.

Queen Nzinga was one of the most interesting rulers who ever walked this planet. A woman in her village prophesied that the ancestors would choose her to be Ngola (ruler) one day. She hung on to that prophetic message like a zebra firmly gripped in the mouth of a lioness. She wanted to fight and hunt growing up with her father, whom she loved dearly. As an archer, she hunted cows, birds, and hippos. This was not your average woman by any means. She was the Serena Williams of her time, taking on all challengers.

Queen Nzinga became an excellent archer and a renowned fierce warrior over time. As a warrior queen and Black female ruler, her reputation and ability to eradicate the plans of foreigners grew. These warriors were bent on enslaving the whole Congo nation and baffled the Portuguese for a long time. After the king passed away, her brother was next on the throne. King Mbandi ended up falling for the European trap for liquor and guns by trading the people of their land into slavery. As a trader of their people, and a backstabber to their father and the entire community, Nzinga no longer viewed him as her brother. It is believed that she was responsible for her brother's death. Between 1600 and 1850, more than five million Africans were kidnapped and transported to Brazil from the Angola region and surrounding areas; that's only ten percent of those who made the horrendous voyage alive. Nzinga was next in line and she wore the crown well.[2]

Queen Anna Nzinga told her father's right-hand man to call her king. She was very popular amongst her people within her village, and everyone's doubts about her favor vanished once the people shouted, "Nzinga, Nzinga! Ngola! Ngola! Rainmaker, Savior of Ndongo, Daughter of the old Ngola!"

Men who refused to come under her rule paid for their insubordination. Many of the chiefs, ministers, and generals under her brother's former rulership refused to support or acknowledge her rulership, simply because they never took orders from a woman. Queen Nzinga sensed that she had to send a message to all of Ndongo, including her enemies from Portugal.

Chief Oyimbu owned an impressive herd of prized cows, which were the livelihood and status symbol for those who could afford them. Without the cows, men were looked down upon. They were nothing in the eyes of the community. A man could not get married, eat properly, perform certain spiritual ceremonies, or negotiate without cows. Queen Nzinga decided to go to the leaders since they wouldn't come to her. The queen and her soldiers paid his village a royal visit and slaughtered all his cows. The next day, Oyimbu came to her with his wife bearing gifts: chickens, goats, baskets, as well as silver and gold bracelets.

They honored Queen Nzinga for her honesty, bravery on the battleground, ability to hunt with the other men, and her regal aura in the face of an immense amount of pressure. Queen Nzinga knew she was a queen from birth; her parents raised her in a village that reminded all the women that they were special.

Today, Queen Nzinga is remembered all over the world. In Angola, she is remembered for her political and diplomatic acumen, great wit, and intelligence, as well as her brilliant military tactics. A major street in Luanda is named after her, and former president Santos dedicated an impressive statue of her in Kinaxixi, Angola in 2002 to celebrate the 27th anniversary of Angola's independence.

Angolan women are often married near her statue. Queen Nzinga knew she was the bomb, and her legacy exemplified that.

MODERN DAY

Isn't it interesting that in a land where many queens were once known as pharaohs, they can't even take a train or walk down a city street without getting their breasts or butt groped? How the heck did modern-day Egypt turn into such a condition? The United Nations Entity for Gender Equality and the Empowerment of Women found that 99.3 percent of Egyptian women have experienced sexual harassment. If that doesn't alarm you, then what if I told you that 82 percent of Egyptian women also reported that they don't feel safe in the streets in 2013?[3]

The country has even created a separate subway train just for women because of the level of ignorance that many of the men there behave at. This was first brought to my attention when I worked for an internet marketing firm, and part of my job was to create sexual harassment videos for attorneys. I was appalled while watching how women were treated in the subway stations, malls, and open streets of Egypt, the land that was once known as Kemet — the jewel of the world. I just couldn't fathom how groups of young and older men would practically rip off any woman's clothes in public shopping centers, like a pack of wolves.

In my opinion, modern-day Egyptian women, and all women around the world, should begin looking at themselves as warrior queens. Start carrying small guns; for instance, you can hide a .22 handgun discreetly under your garments or in your purse. Practice shooting for a couple of weeks so that you won't hesitate to bust those scumbags in the balls if the time comes. I am not a proponent of violence, but I am a true believer of self-defense and protecting my family. Just think, what would Queen Nzinga do?

I know it's important for women of all cultures to know the greatness of other women who lead their country. Therefore, it's important to preserve the true history of Kemet. Women need to see wonderful monuments and statues, such as The Valley of the Queens, temples built in their honor, especially when those women look like them. It gives women, specifically Black women, a sense of pride and a clear sense of identity, which impacts their self-esteem. To know thyself is to love thyself. To love thyself is to truly be able to love others.

There is a Warrior Queen spirit of Nzinga in every woman! All you must do is tap into it.

LIST OF WARRIOR QUEENS FRONTLINE:

Queen Anacaona

Arawak Anacaona (1474-1503) was born in Yaguana, today's town of Legoane, Haiti, and is the first Haitian heroine. Her name "ana" means "golden flower," and "caona," means "gold." The island of Haiti and Dominican Republic were divided into five native tribes or kingdoms. Anacaona became ruler of Xaragua (one of the five kingdoms) when her husband Caonabo, the ruler of the kingdom of Maguna, was deported to Spain in 1494. She succeeded as ruler at the age of 29.

She negotiated with Christopher Columbus and the Spanish exploiters with food and cotton to avoid war. The queen's kindness didn't matter because the foreigners wanted the natural resources and gold, of which the island had abundance. After the death of her brother, the queen had to step up and fight off the Spanish conquerors. Queen Anacaona led her people into battle.

She was eventually caught at a dinner party in her honor. The Spaniards offered her clemency if she would become a concubine. As a woman of dignity who harbored hatred for her enemies, she chose execution instead. Her refusal to cooperate with the Spanish intruders made her a legend. Famous Haitian author Edwidge Danticat wrote the award-winning novel *Anacaona: Golden Flower, Haiti, 1490* in dedication to the brave chieftess; her book will keep the legend of the warrior queen alive. Queen Anacaona's legacy is held with the highest historical significance on the Caribbean island, such as the elite Haitian Generals Toussaint L'Ouverture and Jean Jacques Dessalines.

Hua Mulan

The next warrior Queen I want to present is Hua Mulan from Ancient China (386CE-534CE). The movie *Mulan* was a true story about a young eighteen-year-old girl who fought in place of her old father. In China, it was mandated that each family provide a male to fight in the Chinese army against the invading Mongols and the nomadic tribes. There wasn't a son in her family to join the armed forces to defend their country. This was a position of great pride and honor.

Just like in the Disney animation, Mulan courageously stepped up to the plate. Despite the legend and animated film, she had no small red dragon or talking horse to help her on the battleground (two creative elements that Disney geniuses created). Mulan fought for twelve years. Her skills distinguished her from many of the male soldiers. She had more guts than many of her male counterparts. Could you imagine never intending to fight a battle in your life, and then one day having to make a judgment call to defend your family's honor?

Mulan was offered twelve ranks in those twelve years as a reward for her bravery on the battlefield. Then, according to the legend and

Disney film, Mulan chose to return to a peaceful life with her family. The first legend appeared in a book during the late Ming Dynasty, which lasted from 1368 to 1644 in the 6th century, while a later version of the book expanded on the original poem. There are multiple books, poems, and movies about the life of Mulan.

Harriet Tubman

"I was the conductor of the Underground Railroad for eight years, and I can say what most conductors can't say – I never ran my train off the track and I never lost a passenger." – Harriet Tubman

Born into slavery in 1822, Harriet Tubman (birth name Arminta Ross) became one of the most remarkable women in world history. She tried to escape twice as a teen with her brother. There were countless deaths on Carolina plantations due to the Fugitive Slave Laws in 1850. Harriet helped more than 300 slaves reach their freedom, including her mom and dad, during the night without any map or guide other than the North Star. She was so good that Maryland planters offered $40,000 for her capture.

As an adult, she took 19 trips back and forth to the eastern shore of Maryland through the muddy swamps and crossed the Delaware River. Then, they walked an additional 500 miles into Ontario, Canada where the runaway slaves would be FREE at last!

Growing up, she watched her mom, Harriet "Rit" Green, hide her brother from a slave owner, whom she even threatened to fight if he touched her son. The apple didn't fall too far from the tree. Incidents like these planted seeds in young Harriet that she could one day fight back against anyone, especially her oppressors. As a strong Christian and woman of faith, she fought to keep her faith alive, believing that God would deliver her people from a life of toil.

Harriet was a first-generation slave in the United States of America, and she wanted to make sure that she was the last. Her action to free her people was a 'selfless' act of courage. She was conscious about the future of those who were enslaved, and she did something about it. As a true queen, Harriet changed their destiny.

Harriet rejected the teachings of the New Testament because it urged Africans to be obedient, and she found guidance in the Old Testament through the stories of deliverance. Multiple slave-owners whom she was hired to serve beat her numerous times. Early in her life, she suffered a severe head wound after being hit with a heavy metal weight. The injury caused disabling epileptic seizures, head-aches, powerful visions, and dream experiences, which occurred throughout her life.

Whenever I hear the name Harriet Tubman, I feel a sense of courageousness. Harriet put it all on the line to free her people in the Underground Railroad. She was an African American abolitionist, humanitarian, and Union spy during the American Civil War. It is estimated that she rescued 700 people during the raid at Combahee Ferry. The network of abolitionists and safe houses created what is known as the Underground Railroad. For a very long time, I thought it was an underground tunnel that went from the southern slave states all the way to Canada.

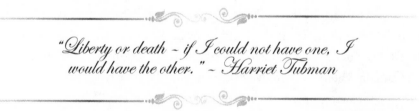

"Liberty or death – if I could not have one, I would have the other." – Harriet Tubman

Two of America's strongest Black leaders spoke highly of her valor. The late great Fredrick Douglass even gave Harriet praise in a letter in his autobiography in 1868. Booker T. Washington mentioned her name when he delivered the keynote address. She was nicknamed "General Tubman," and "Moses" because of her strength and tenacity to uphold her promise to save as many enslaved Africans as possible. In the eyes of her people, Harriet Tubman was a champion freedom fighter! A hundred and fifty years later, her name still shines like gold whenever it is mentioned. Her spirit continues to motivate those who hear about her heroism.

How far would you go to free your people from slavery: mental slavery, economic slavery, or modern-day slavery? Are you willing to free the minds of our youth and release them from the captivity of prison cells sweeping across many countries? Are you willing to sacrifice some of your 'selfies' to read a book that will liberate your mind, body, and spirit so that you can share your newfound wisdom? The bravery and wisdom of Harriet Tubman is exactly what is needed to make a difference and empower us today.

Winnie Mandela

One of the most controversial women in the world's history is Winnie Mandela, most notably known as the first wife of the world-renowned Nelson Mandela. Her birth name was Nomzamo Winifred Zanyiwe Madikizela — Mother of the South African Nation. She was controversial due to her fiery spirit and no-holds-barred tongue. Mrs. Mandela chose Nelson Mandela because of the voltage of energy he carried with him. She read all about him in the newspapers. She felt his courageous spirit as a young attorney in South Africa's apartheid, and when she saw him speak about his vision for the future of Africa, her heart connected with his energy and passion for their people. She knew he was powerful enough to sustain her dynamic character. Eventually, they married in 1957, one year after he met her at the bus stop on her way to school.

Everything about Winnie Mandela resonated strength (her name means "one who tries"). She was the first Black professional social welfare worker in South Africa, devoted to serving those in need. She used her energy and skills to fight for justice and equality for her people. Winnie and Nelson encouraged each other throughout the hard times when Nelson was imprisoned, and even during the time they both were incarcerated. He would constantly remind her that she was the mother of the country — Mother of the Nation.

Coretta Scott King

Coretta Scott King was an American civil rights activist and the wife of the world-renowned civil rights leader, Martin Luther King, Jr. They gave birth to four children, and they also gave birth to the Civil Rights Act of 1964.

They had something great to fight for — equality. During most of Dr. King's marches, he was accompanied by Coretta's benevolent smile. Her strength as a woman, a Black woman, resonated throughout the world. Black folks were at war against the government and fighting the ignorance of most of the country's white population.

The leaders of the Civil Rights Movement, and hundreds of thousands of protesters, risked putting their lives on the line for the right to vote. The difference between the women of the 1960s and the women of the new millennium is that they had something admirable to fight for during their time. They fought for equal rights for their families, present and future.

In Dr. King's own words, he stated: "I am trying to do what is right. I'm losing courage. I am trying to do what is right." He received many troubling death threats everywhere that he went, even at his humble abode. I can imagine Coretta stepping up to the plate during this time to uplift his spirits.

Dr. King also spoke very highly of his wife for her support.

"I am indebted to my wife Coretta, without whose love, sacrifices, and loyalty, and neither life nor work would bring fulfillment.

She has given me words of consolation when I needed them and a well-ordered home where Christian love is a reality."

As a man on a mission and a woman of courage, Dr. King and his First Lady knew what was at stake. Failure to complete their mission, which was to get the Civil Rights Act passed in Congress, had devastating consequences. Black people underwent a miserable time in the United States and had difficulty gaining jobs, community resources, or fair treatment from law authorities. Regardless of the risk, I believe they continued to push forward because they lost the fear of death. Many people believe this is when one begins to truly enjoy their life and their loved ones.

Could you imagine the pressure that Mrs. King had to endure during the turbulent days of the 1950s and 1960s? She insisted on being alongside her man during the hectic racial tensions despite his wishes for her to stay home to raise the children.

It behooves you to follow suit of the women of Ashanti to Coretta Scott King by inspiring your king to be the warrior for your family and community. Today, women can fight for their kings!

Dear Queen,

We create fear when we use our energy to focus on the end result we hope to avoid. Fear is an illusion, and a Warrior Queen will make sure that her man remembers that during times of battle.

BONUS CHAPTERS

THE BLACK CAT THEORY

*A*t some point in time and space, Black cats were like the celebrities of the animal kingdom, where they were held in high esteem and were highly favored pets. They were known for protecting people from various evil spirits and entities. In

208

fact, the only thing negative about Black cats is a person's perception of them, which was created by those in our society whose intention was to create a gloomy cloud of bad luck about them. Ultimately, this gave them a negative connotation by making them high on the list of superstitions. The origin of these myths surrounding Black cats, including why a Black cat walking near you is considered bad luck, was created by those who were familiar with their worth, prominence, and value. They wanted the masses to become disconnected from them and to fear them at the same time; people usually stay away from what they are terrified of.

The symbol of the Kemetians is a Black female cat-headed deity called Bastet. Her name means "she of the perfume jar." She was highly revered as the kindly goddess of all pets and household cats and also as the war-like lion-headed goddess. Bastet was a goddess in the ancient Egyptian religion, worshiped as early as the 2nd Dynasty (2890 BCE). She was the guardian of earth and home, and here is the kicker: she was the symbol of good luck not bad luck, as we were led to believe since we were children in cartoons, books, and movies. Why, you ask? Buckle your seatbelts. The feminine energy has and will always be regarded as sacred in Ancient African High Culture Civilizations.

The Black cat was also associated with the Nubian lioness War Goddess, Sekhmet, whom they called the sphinx, which the general populace of the Nile Valley highly revered. Notice that I've mentioned two female African deities that predate any and all religions practiced today, which we'll get into a little deeper. You will find out why, once upon a time, it was (and still is) believed that "The Black Woman Is God." This concept was wholeheartedly believed by mainly people of African descent, but those that are well-versed in real history will agree.

We've also been taught that the Black cat is associated with witches, which is also false. This was done to diminish the confidence and image of African women, who the people of antiquity believed to be gods on earth. Most importantly, they wanted to destroy the image of the family structure such as the original trinity — Queen Auset, King Ausar, and their son Heru. Queen Auset's name became known as Isis to the Graeco-Romans (Greco-Roman), who invaded and occupied Kemet, and many great African dynasties, causing the decline of these societies. "From 323 to 30 B.C.E., Lower Egypt (Falcon Head Crowned Pharaohs) was occupied by Macedonian-Greeks who set up a strong-hold in the area known as Alexandria (after the Greek military leader and plunderer)," says Danita Redd, educator and holistic counselor, in the classic book *Black Women of Antiquity*. The admiration for the deity Queen Auset (Isis) was so intoxicating that it created a huge cult following.

Initially, the Romans began the worshipping of Isis with such zeal that the popularity of the sect made its way into Italy and Sicily. In time, Isis shrines were ordered to be torn down and were outlawed by Augustus in Rome and Tiberius (Roman Emperor from 14 AD to 37 AD), who persecuted the priests. In their eyes, it was difficult to worship the gods of the people and land that they were exploiting and pillaging, which is still going on today throughout the continent of Africa. This was the beginning of the worldwide plot to destroy the image of a *Black Woman as God* and the power of the sovereignty of the *naturally rich* African countries. This was done in order have power over the minds of the Africans. Spirituality and religious beliefs have always been pivotal to the everyday lives of most civilized people. This act would successfully hinder the image of loving, thriving Black families. This made the men weaker by getting them to join in on the disrespect and over-sexualizing the very source of their energy and power — the Black woman.

As in the 21st century, image is everything. From how we see ourselves now, and where we see ourselves in the future, image is vital to our goal setting or the lack thereof. A perfect example is actress Esther Elizabeth Rolle, who was a Bahamian American born in

Pompano Beach, FL. She's best known for her role as Florida Evans in the hit family 1970s sitcom *Good Times*, co-starring the stern John Amos, the flamboyant Ja'net Dubois, young Janet Jackson, militant Ralph Carter, the gorgeous Bern Nadette Stanis, and the hilarious Jimmie Walker. The directors of the show originally didn't want a Black man acting as a husband in the home, but Ms. Rolle fought tooth and nail, and even refused to be on the show. She felt that, by not having a husband on the show, it was promoting single motherhood on national television to millions of viewers. She knew that her people needed to see the *image* of a Black family unit loving and caring for each other, just like any other culture does. If you had the power to choose the plot of the show, would you project a positive image of a family or a broken home? All cultures need families working and supporting one another. It's critical on so many levels.

The powers that be understood the power of images, symbols, and unity. Mother Africa has been seen for a very long time as a rich pie filled with precious stones, gold, human cargo, and oil to be divided amongst world powers, such as Britain, France, Germany, Italy, Portugal, the United States, and Spain. Ironically, in many churches throughout Europe, and behind closed doors, priests and popes of the Roman Catholic churches continue to worship and kiss the African goddess Auset.

"The statues and paintings of her are called the Black Madonna, 'Mother of God,' 'Great Mother,' 'Immaculate Virgin,' to whom women prayed for forgiveness of sexual sins," says Danita Redd. A few other titles given to the African Goddess were 'Queen of Heaven,' 'Mother God,' 'Star of the Sea,' and 'Our Lady.'

Furthermore, the witches were associated with the Black cat due to the fact that Black women of antiquity were the wisest women in the world and known for their clairvoyance, especially women from the Kushite Empire (Ethopia), such as Queen of Sheba, Makeda. Most of the Druid priestesses, ancient religious leaders of Celtic

Societies (Iron Age Europe 1000 BC), had a Black cat as a house pet. The Black cat goes against the status quo of the popular religion, such as Christian mythology, Catholics, etc., so therefore propaganda had to be created to destroy the image.

Additionally, King James VI of Scotland, who in 1603 became James I of England (creator of KJV Bible in 1601), was a witch-hunting fanatic and a devout woman hater. Many people left Britain and those exiled pilgrims from England ran away to the Americas, a.k.a. colonies. Christian mythology and Druidic mythology clashed due to different ideologies, and this is part of where the concept of Black cats being "bad luck" came from, since many of the Druid priestess had them as pets. Both of these religions are referred to as mythologies because of the lack of tangible power — it's all based on what one believes gives them a connection to The Creator. Astrology, science of agriculture, and the science of mathematics can be seen and proven and were originated by ancient African civilizations. African women were always associated with Mother Nature due to their expertise in the science of agriculture, which involved the protection of the animals.

What's more, White women who were taught by African women were highly feared for their knowledge; this automatically made the White women of Europe smarter than most men at the time, which spelled grave danger. At the time, promoting your intelligence and skills in natural remedies with herbs and plants was dangerous. Women had to dull their shine, or face possible execution during this dark time in Europe. As stated earlier in this literature, you can tell a lot about a country by the way the girls and women are treated. It makes perfect sense why in medieval Europe they fell into *The Dark Ages* — they were constantly dimming the brilliance of their women. God forbid, but if you were both a woman and intelligent, you were labeled a cunning woman and, even worse, a witch.

Having said that, the Salem Witch Trials in colonial Massachusetts took place from February 1692 to May 1693. The broomstick and the witch were synonymous because most women took care of the home and were often sweeping. The caveman mentality of European men desiring their woman naked, barefoot, cooking, and pregnant was a common practice; in Africa this wasn't the way of life. As a matter of fact, their matriarchal society was the exact opposite. No wonder there were three Golden Ages in Africa, while Europe was fighting to survive in the Dark Ages. It all stems from the source and creative energy force of women.

I've seen people run in terror when a Black cat walks by them. Little did they know that the Black feline is actually a symbol of good luck and blessings. Now when I see one of these friendly felines, I smile. My spirit embraces their presence as a present.

In conclusion, the next time you see a Black cat — wave and smile. They may smile back at you.

42 LAWS OF MAAT

1. I have not committed sin.

2. I have not committed robbery with violence.

3. I have not stolen.

4. I have not slain men or women.

5. I have not stolen food.

6. I have not swindled offerings.

7. I have not stolen from God/Goddess.

8. I have not told lies.

9. I have not carried away food.

10. I have not cursed.

11. I have not closed my ears to truth.

12. I have not committed adultery.

13. I have not made anyone cry.

14. I have not felt sorrow without reason.

15. I have not assaulted anyone.

16. I am not deceitful.

17. I have not stolen anyone's land.

18. I have not been an eavesdropper.

19. I have not falsely accused anyone.

20. I have not been angry without reason.

21. I have not seduced anyone's wife.

22. I have not polluted myself.

23. I have not terrorized anyone.

24. I have not disobeyed the Law.

25. I have not been exclusively angry.

26. I have not cursed God/Goddess.

27. I have not behaved with violence.

28. I have not caused disruption of peace.

29. I have not acted hastily or without thought.

30. I have not overstepped my boundaries of concern.

31. I have not exaggerated my words when speaking.

32. I have not worked evil.

33. I have not used evil thoughts, words, or deeds.

34. I have not polluted the water.

35. I have not spoken angrily or arrogantly.

36. I have not cursed anyone in thought, word, or deeds.

37. I have not placed myself on a pedestal.

38. I have not stolen what belongs to God/Goddess.

39. I have not stolen from or disrespected the deceased.

40. I have not taken food from a child.

41. I have not acted with insolence.

42. I have not destroyed property belonging to God/Goddess.

Ma'at, or MAAT refers to the ancient Egyptian concepts of truth, balance, order, harmony, law, morality, peace, and justice. It pertains to the personification of these concepts as a goddess regulating the stars, seasons, and the actions of both mortals and deities, who set the order of the universe from chaos at the moment of creation.

It's also known as the 42 Laws of MAAT, or 42 Negative Confessions, or 42 Admonition to Goddess Maat, or 42 Declarations of Innocence or Admonitions of Maát, 42 Laws of Maat of Ancient Egypt, or the Laws of the Goddess Maat.

AVAILABLE BOOKS, PRODUCTS, AND PROGRAMS COMING SOON: THE EMPIRE

- Inspirational Autobiography: *The Courage to Believe* – Available on iTunes, Amazon, Paperback and eBooks.

- *7 Types of Queens, Kings Desire* – 2017 *7 Types of Kings, Queens Desire* – 2018

- Autobiography: *The Courage to Believe: Never Give Up* – November 2017 (French edition coming this Fall.)

- Documentary: *The Courage to Believe: Never Give Up* – July 2017

- Stage Play: *The Courage to Believe* – Available Now

- Children's book: *King Kevin's Courage* – July 1, 2018

- Support: Courage To Believe International, Inc. A 501(c) 3 nonprofit youth mentoring organization founded in 2014 by the author: C2B Chess Club & Youth Mentoring Program. Annual Black-on-Black Crime Solutions Panel Movement. For more information, please visit the website: www.thecouragetobelieve.com

LIFE SKILLS WORKSHOPS/ LECTURES:

How to Find the King & Queen in You

How to Stay Focused While in The Fires of Life

Black Authors That Paved the Way

History of the Caribbean

Avoid Police Brutality

Create Your Future

Black-on-Black Crime Solutions

10 Ways to Find Courage

Get Your Book Published NOW!

FOLLOW ME AND GET INSPIRED ON SOCIAL NETWORKS:

Facebook: "7 Types of Queens, Kings Desire"
Twitter: @7Queens7Kings
Instagram: @7Queens7Kings
Google +: Kevin Dorival
YouTube: Kevin Dorival
Black Planet: @Courage2Believe
Goodreads: Courage2Believe
Tumblr: Courage2Believe
Twitter: @Courage2Believe
Instagram: @Courage2Believe

If you enjoyed the book, please let your opinions be heard on Amazon.com, BN.com, iTunes Books, Goodreads.com, and wherever books are sold. Demand that *7 Types of Queens, Kings Desire* be included at your local bookstore/library.

For Speaking, Coaching, Marketing Services, or Queen Workshop Inquires, contact me at: 7queens7kings@gmail.com.

Should you find mistakes in this book, or have suggestions and/or comments, please contact me at: 7queens7kings@gmail.com - Subject: Book Advice.

Want to stay up-to-date with what's going on in my career, or the latest projects? Sign up for my newsletter: 7queens7kings@gmail.com - Include "Signup" Subject in the line.

HOTEP & BLESSINGS TO YOU &
YOUR MARRIAGE TO COME!

BIBLIOGRAPHY

Chapter 1

1. Haimerl, Amy. (2015). The fastest-growing group of entrepreneurs in America. *Fortune.* June 29, 2015 http://fortune.com/2015/06/29/Black-women-entrepreneurs/

2. Durant, Will. *Our Oriental Heritage. Story of Civilization. Fine Communications.* 1935. Print.

3. Dr. Barashango, Ishakamusa. *Afrikan Woman the Original Guardian Angel. 1989.*

4. *The Valley of the Queens* by King Kevin Dorival.

5. Diop, Dr. Cheikh Anta. *The Cultural Unity of Black Africa: The Domains of Matriarchy & of Patriarchy in Classical Antiquity.* Mass Market. 2000. Print.

6. Dr. Barashango, Ishakamusa. *Afrikan Woman the Original Guardian Angel.* 1989.

Chapter 2

1. Diop, Dr. Cheikh Anta. *The Cultural Unity of Black Africa: The Domains of Matriarchy & of Patriarchy in Classical Antiquity.* Mass Market. 2000. Print.

2. Dr. Barashango, Ishakamusa. *Afrikan Woman the Original Guardian Angel.* 1989.

3. Dr. Myles, Monroe. *7 Principles of an Eagle.*

4. Borgatti, Jean. *Race and History: African Influence on Christianity.* http://www.raceandhistory.com/historicalviews/20122001.htm

5. *Osiris and the Egyptian Resurrection*, Volume 2 by Sir Ernest Alfred Wallis Budge.

6. Barbara G. Walker, scholar and author of *Woman's Encyclopedia of Myths and Secrets.*

Chapter 3

1. *"The Black Man's Guide to Understanding the Black Woman"* book and lecture by Shahrazad Ali.

2. Dr. Llia Afrika. *"Holistic Afrikan Health"*. *Eworld.* 2004. Print.

3. "8 Worst Foods for Your Digestion" – *Huffington Post*

4. *Will Fast-Food Franchises Ever Die?* Great American Cookies Franchise. 2015. http://www.greatamericancookiesfranchise. com/will-fast-food-franchises-ever-die/

5. Obama, Michelle. *Michelle Obama, In Her Own Words.* 2008.

6. *"First Lady Michelle Obama"*, *Associated Press*, May 28, 2007.

7. Lewis, Hunter. *"The First Lady of Food: Michelle Obama"*. *Cooking Light.* February 9, 2015. http://www.cookinglight.com/food/everyday-menus/michelle-obama-first-lady-of-food

8. Courtesy of Statista.com 2014.

9. Dr. Sertima, Ivan Van. *Black Women of Antiquity.* 1984.

Chapter 5

1. "Black Crime Rates: What Happens When Numbers Aren't Neutral," *Huffington Post*, 2015

2. Zarya, Valentina. *"This is Why Women Are the Fastest-Growing Prison Population,"* by *Fortune.com*. December 10, 2015 http://fortune.com/2015/12/10/prison-reform-women/

3. *Women's Liberation and the African Freedom Struggle"* by Thomas Sankara.

4. *"Nebuchadnezzar: The Head of God"* by Joseph R. Chambers.

5. Note: King Nebuchadnezzar: was the one they said created the Hanging Gardens in the sixth century B.C. There's conflicting evidence of this however that a king three hundred miles north of his Neo-Babylonian empire. Assyrian King Sennacherib. We know this thanks to Dr. Stephanie Dalley, an honorary researcher and part of the Oriental Institute at England's Oxford University. The Hanging Gardens was labeled one of the Seven Wonders of the Ancient World.

Chapter 6

1. Erich Fromm, Peter D. Kramer *"The Art of Loving,"* Erich Fromm. Harper Perennial Modern Classics. November 21, 2006.

2. Dr. Barashango, Ishakamusa. *Afrikan Woman the Original Guardian Angel*. 1989.

Chapter 7

1. *Indians of The Western Range*. Time Life Books. 1996. Print.

2. Bryant, Taylor. *How The Beauty Industry Has Failed Black Women*. Refinery 29. February 27, 2016. http://www.refinery29.com/2016/02/103964/Black-hair-care-makeup-business

3. Winfrey, Oprahy. *The Moment Phylicia Rashad First Felt Beautiful*. 7 HARPO PRODUCTIONS, INC. 1987 http://www.oprah.com/oprahshow/the-moment-phylicia-rashad-realized-she-was-truly-beautiful#ixzz4abnC9VyT

Chapter 8

1. *More Than A Hero: Muhammad Ali's Life Lessons Through His Daughter's Eyes* by Hana Ali. 2000.

2. The Fortney Encyclical Black History: The World's True Black History.

3. Griffith, Florence "Flo-Jo" Delorez. *"Flo-Jo Talks About The Importance of Physical Fitness"*. *Jets Magazine*. June 1997. Print.

4. Dr. Llia Afrika. "Holistic Afrikan Health". *Eworld*. 2004. Print.

5. Johnson, Dale Albert. *Forty Days on the Holy Mountain*. Lulu. 2016

6. Encyclopedia Britannica.com. Josephine Baker

7. Windsor, Rudolph R. *From Babylon to Timbuktu: A History of the Ancient Black Races*. Windsor Golden Series. 2006.

Chapter 9

1. The Pearl Harbor attack, as remember by the nurses who were there. 12/2/2016. Army.Mil.com.

2. Spencer, Diana. *Diana Revealed The Princess No One Know*. Heart of the Matter. February 14, 1997. BBC1.

Chapter 11

1. Dr. Llia Afrika. "Holistic Afrikan Health". *Eworld.* 2004. Print.

2. Vitale, Joe. *Hypnotic Writing – How To Seduce and Persuade Customers With Only Your Words.* 2007. Print.

Chapter 12

1. Diop, Dr. Cheikh Anta. *The Cultural Unity of Black Africa: The Domains of Matriarchy & of Patriarchy in Classical Antiquity.* Mass Market. 2000. Print.

2. "Nubiah" July 28, 2015 by Thomas Jones.

3. Moral Epidemic of Egypt: 99% of Women Are Sexually Harassed

Bonus Chapter

1. Dr. Amos Wilson, "Black Male, Black Female Relationships." 1992.

2. *25 Extremely Strange Wedding Traditions.* 11/24/2014 by David Pegg. List25.com